STUDENT IMPACT

Volume Two Small Group Resources

Compassion for Lost People

Twelve Lessons That Will Change Your Friends' Lives

Bo Boshers
Erin Frazier and Tricia Murphy

ZondervanPublishingHouse
Grand Rapids, Michigan
A Division of HarperCollins*Publishers*

Willow Creek Resources

I would like to dedicate this curriculum to each of you with a shepherd's heart who has been called by God to serve high school students. I pray that the small groups on these pages will be a powerful resource for gathering students together and putting them on the path to becoming fully devoted followers of Christ. May God richly bless you for following the call He's placed on your heart to impact the lives of students ... you are making a difference.

Serving together, one life at a time,
Bo

Compassion for Lost People

Requests for information should be addressed to:
ZondervanPublishingHouse
Grand Rapids, Michigan 49530

ISBN: 0–310–20126–8

Interior design by Jack Rogers

Printed in the United States of America

98 99 00 01 02 03 04 /❖ ML/ 10 9 8 7 6 5 4

CONTENTS

ACKNOWLEDGMENTS

I would like to recognize and express my thanks to those who were instrumental in making this project happen.

To Tricia Murphy, who used her creativity, devotion, and desire to capture God's Truth for the result of moving students practically to find the love of Christ. Thank you for your friendship and sensitivity.

To Troy Murphy, my lifelong friend, who used his artistic gifts to help create the right format for sharing this resource. Thank you for your devotion to this project; I love running the race with you.

To Erin Frazier, who joined the team through her willingness to take a step of adventure in using her gift of writing. Thank you for your contribution and promptness; I hope there are more projects for us to do together in the future.

To Lynette Rubin, my friend and assistant, for her availability, support, and willingness to adjust when I needed it. I could not have done this without you.

To Dave Lambert, Rachel Boers, Jane Vogel, and their teams at Zondervan, who gave us understanding, support, patience, and direction in developing this project. Thank you for your time and energy.

And to the Willow Creek Association team, for the many people who were involved in making this desire for small group curriculum a reality. Thank you for the privilege of doing this project with you. Together we have all seen a dream come true.

Introduction

You are holding in your hands an exciting tool! It's not every day that you can find a tool that will:

- assist you in touching the lives of high school students with whom you are involved—as a full-time, part-time, or volunteer youth leader;
- equip you to talk to your students in ways that will allow them to experience God in more intimate ways;
- change the way you develop small groups in your student ministry.

Walk through the next few pages and catch the vision for this tool that will help you make a difference in the lives of high school students.

The next few pages are devoted to sharing a vision for small groups in student ministry. You will discover how small groups can most effectively be used to bring about life changes and specifically how to implement small groups using the experiences in this book. Take plenty of time to reflect on the impact these opportunities for community and growth can have on the students whose lives you influence.

WHY SMALL GROUPS?

Change—The Purpose of Small Groups

Small groups are essential to the development of spiritual life in those who want to be fully devoted followers of Christ. They are essential because community, growth, sharing, and discipleship happen in the context of a group. In Student Impact, the high school ministry of Willow Creek Community Church in Barrington, Illinois, we refer to our small groups as D-Teams (with the "D" representing the Greek word *Delta,* meaning "change.") Our mission is simply to turn irreligious high school students into fully devoted followers of Christ.

To accomplish this mission, Student Impact is based on a seven-step strategy. Everything we do fits into this strategy:

1. Integrity Friendship
   The process begins as we challenge our core students to build "relational bridges" with their non-Christian friends.
2. Verbal Witness
   After students have built credible friendships with their non-Christian friends, we teach them to look for opportunities to explain and discuss their relationship with Christ.
3. Supplemental Witness: Providing a Service for Seekers
   Student Impact, our service for seekers, is designed to nurture students' spiritual interest by introducing them to the message of Christ in a contemporary and relevant way. Impact is intended to be used as a tool by our core in reaching their non-Christian friends by supplementing their ongoing witness.
4. Spiritual Challenge
   At this stage of their friendship, we teach our core students to ask pointed questions that intentionally challenge their friends to consider the claims of Christ. We believe that once a seeker has spent time listening to God's Word and observing fully devoted Christian students, he will

discover through the conviction of the Holy Spirit his need for a personal relationship with Jesus Christ.

5. Integration into the Body
   Student Insight, our worship service for believers, is designed to mature the believer on the trek toward full devotion to Christ. Insight provides believers with an opportunity to participate in corporate worship and to listen to expository Bible teaching.
6. Discipleship Through Small Groups
   Small groups provide a discipleship atmosphere. From this small group comes accountability, encouragement, and support, as well as Biblical teaching through learning experiences.
7. Ownership
   At this stage of spiritual development, students are taking an active role in service within the church. Through both financial giving and using their spiritual gifts, they are owning their part of the Lord's work. A student now steps forward and takes the role of evangelist within his own circle of influence and thus begins a third spiritual generation. This occurs as he takes his non-Christian friends through the same seven steps he traveled.

The vision of Student Impact is to create a unique community of students and leaders committed to letting God

- change their lives;
- change their friends' lives;
- build the church; and
- impact the world.

The four volumes of small group experiences, *Walking with Christ*, *Compassion for Lost People*, *Learning to Serve*, and *A Lifelong Calling*, are written with these four values (we call them "waves" of ministry) in mind. This book of experiences focuses on the second wave of life change: sharing Christ with friends. Once a student has accepted Christ and has a personal relationship with Him, he or she can't help but want to share the truth of Christ with friends. This volume will assist you in equipping students to engage their friends in conversation about Jesus and to recognize how evangelism works in their daily lives.

For a fuller development of how small groups fit into the vision and mission of student ministry, see *Student Ministry for the 21st Century: Transforming Your Youth Group into a Vital Student Ministry* by Bo Boshers with Kim Anderson (Zondervan, 1997).

Authenticity—Leading by Example

As the leader of small group life, your role is not only to teach the Word of God but to be an example to your students. It's more than talking. It's living in the moment with students, thinking the way they think, asking questions that allow them to reflect on their world, creating an environment that provides opportunities for uninterrupted community and soul-searching. These moments are about helping students take the time to look at Christ and grow to be more like Him. It's about life change.

In Student Impact, D-Teams meet every other week. But our walk with Christ is lived out daily. Today's students are looking for leaders who live authentic lives in Christ. As a leader, you not only facilitate the D-Team experiences, but you work to help students view the world from God's perspective each day. The greatest lesson students learn is not from these materials but from your life. This can happen only through your commitment of time, prayer, and preparation. The D-Team experiences in this book will serve as the basis for group interaction, but the key to fully devoted followership is allowing God to work through you so that students experience Him.

If you're unfamiliar with the D-Team format, take a few minutes to read the following overview.

HOW TO USE THIS BOOK

For each small group meeting, you'll find Leader's Notes that will guide you through your preparation and actual leading of the group experience, and Student Notes that you can photocopy and distribute to your students to use during your time together. The Student Notes are perforated so that you can take them out of the book and photocopy the two pages back-to-back, then fold them to form a four-page booklet that your students can slip easily into their Bibles. (You'll notice that the page numbers in the Student Notes look out of order when they are unassembled.) Encourage your students to take their notes home, perhaps filing them in a notebook or binder, so they can look back at what they've learned throughout their small group experiences.

The Leader's Notes contain all the information in the Student Notes plus the following features to help you prepare and lead your students.

Unit Introduction

Each unit begins with an introduction that includes the Leader Focus and Big Picture. The Leader Focus will help you begin thinking about the unit theme from a new perspective. In the Big Picture, you'll find a brief description of the values and objectives for each unit as well as the D-Team experiences themselves. You'll also get your first look at the Unit Memory Verse. Each unit builds on the one before, but you can also use the units independently if that's more appropriate for your time frame or the needs of your particular students. You'll notice that the lessons within each unit are numbered independent of the other units to give you this flexibility.

Before the D-Team Experience

Each session has an easy-to-use summary outline that will help you see the D-Team experience at a glance.

- *Leader Devotion*—To impact students at the deepest level, there can be no mistaking the value of a leader's personal authenticity. The heart of the leader is key. This section will challenge you to recall personal experiences and gain new insights that you can share with your students. This mini-devotion will prepare you for the role of leadership.
- *Student Focus*—This section provides the leader with the rationale for the D-Team experience. It provides clarification on what a student can expect if he or she is committed to this experience and the truths to be learned. It may also provide an opening discussion question.
- *Unit Memory Verse*—Only four memory verses appear in each volume. When students focus on memorizing one verse per unit, they will truly have ownership of that verse and can apply it to their lives on a daily basis.
- *Practical Impact*—We believe students learn best when they experience God's truth, not just talk about it. Each Practical Impact section outlines ways for students not only to hear the Word of God, but to experience it.
- *Materials Needed*—Here you will find a list of everything you need to bring to the D-Team experience. Student Notes are provided for each D-Team experience and can be duplicated back-to-back for your D-Team members. Encourage your students to keep these notes in a binder so they can look back on what they've learned.
- *Special Preparation*—In this section, you will find detailed instructions to help you prepare for your D-Team experience. Phone contacts, letters, reproducible handouts, suggestions about advance phone contacts and letters, and other ideas for resources will help ensure that your D-Team experience goes smoothly.
- *Environment*—Because students are sometimes more able to freely experience God outside the context of four walls, each D-Team experience offers two options. Option 1 works in any setting, while Option 2 moves the experience outside a normal meeting room to an environment that has been created specially for the D-Team. Option 2 takes time and thought on the part of the leader, but it can set up a D-Team experience in a very powerful way. Explore your options. Figure out what freedom you have in this area. Depending on the size or structure of your student ministry, the environment can be established in different ways. If a large number of students meet together before they divide into different D-Teams, a master teacher approach can help to establish the environment by "painting a picture," then dismissing students.

Leading the D-Team Experience (60 min.)

Your entire D-Team experience should last approximately 60 minutes. It's divided into four sections: Get Started (5 minutes), The Experience (40 minutes), Reflection (5 minutes), and Make an Impact (10 minutes). Questions and Scriptures that are ***bold-face and italic*** in your Leader's Notes are duplicated in the Student Notes.

Get Started (5 min.)
During the first five minutes of the first D-Team experience of each unit, you will help your students: preview the objectives of the unit; understand the Unit Memory Verse; spend some time in prayer; and discover what to expect in this D-Team experience. In the next two D-Team experiences of each unit, you will use this time to review assignments and challenges from the previous D-Team experiences, encourage student-led prayer, and share objectives for the new D-Team experience.

The Experience (40 min.)
This forty-minute section is broken down into several steps to help you lead the experience. This is the practical work and discussion section for the students. You'll find step-by-step instructions along with discussion questions, Bible study, activities, and various practical exercises. Feel free to insert your own thoughts and insights—things God showed you during your Leader Devotion time as well as in your general preparation for the D-Team experience.

Reflection (5 min.)
This five-minute portion of the experience will help your group members solidify the truths they have learned as they reflect individually on the experience. Encourage your D-Team members to truly invest in this section. Model for them the value of reflection as you work through the questions listed here. Don't be afraid of the silence of reflection as opportunities for growth are being formed in students' minds! Model openness in your own personal application, but especially encourage your D-Team members to share their ideas on how to apply the truths in their lives. Use the Summary Statements to reinforce the truths the students have learned.

Make an Impact (10 min.)
During the last ten minutes of your D-Team experience, you have the opportunity to challenge your students to make personal applications of the principles they have experienced. Don't forget to seek God's guidance for each of your students.

- ... *In Your Life*—Students like to be challenged. This section allows you to offer some sort of assignment and challenge to your D-Team members. Let them know they have a choice in accepting the challenges. Make it inviting to commit, but not easy. Remind your students that it takes training to develop godly character (1 Tim. 4:7b-8) that will bear fruit.

- ... *With Accountability*—In this section, you will encourage each student to choose another person in the D-Team as an accountability partner. Together, they will work on the Unit Memory Verse. In addition, accountability partners will have opportunities to share their responses to assignments and challenges.

- *Prayer*—Be sure to close the D-Team experience in prayer. Model the value of prayer by upholding it before and after each D-Team experience. Invite your students to pray as they are comfortable. Explore this opportunity to pray in community with your D-Team members if you find that they are hesitant to pray aloud. You may ask certain students to pray for specific areas as you sense the development of community and safety.

FOLLOW UP
If you have more than one small group, you can use the Shepherding Summary Form (page 111) to enable communication between D-Team leaders and the ministry director. Duplicate this form and have each D-Team Leader in your student ministry fill it out after each D-Team experience. Simply indicate brief responses to the questions in each section. Over time, this process will assist you in accountability, opportunities for encouragement, record-keeping for D-Team member information, and direction-setting for your student ministry leader.

RIGHT HERE, RIGHT NOW

STUDENT IMPACT

Unit 1 Introduction

LEADER FOCUS

Read Matthew 5:14–15. Although these are simple verses, the message is something we should constantly be striving to achieve. Ask yourself: *What are some situations where I am tempted to hide my light? Why?* Think of times when it is easier to shine your light and why. As you prepare to speak to your students about the urgency of spreading the Gospel, spend some time in prayer about your own life. What can you do to keep your light aglow? How can you be sure you are taking advantage of every opportunity to witness? Ask God to fill your heart with a sense of urgency.

BIG PICTURE

Unit Overview

In Unit 1 you will focus on accomplishing one goal—to fill your students with a sense of urgency to evangelize to the world. Your students will see clearly that everyone needs God. They will come to realize that, because Christians have the answer for a sick world, they must share that answer.

1. People Need God

During this D-Team experience, your students will discover the first urgent reason we are called to evangelize: People need God. They will make this discovery by studying two supporting truths:

Truth #1: God created everyone in His own image.
Truth #2: Everyone is lost without God.

2. We Have the Answer

During this D-Team experience, your students will discover the second urgent reason we are called to evangelize: We have the answer. They will make this discovery by doing two things:

Action Step #1: *Know* that we have the only answer.
Action Step #2: *Tell* the answer to everyone.

3. Life Is Short

During this D-Team experience, your students will discover the third urgent reason we are called to evangelize: Life is short. They will make this discovery as they identify and believe the following facts:

Unit 1 Introduction

Fact #1: Time does not stop.
Fact #2: Everyone dies.
Fact #3: People will spend eternity in heaven or hell.
Fact #4: There are people we may only see once in our lives.
Fact #5: The time is now!

Unit Memory Verse

"Be wise in the way you act toward outsiders; make the most of every opportunity. Let your conversation be always full of grace, seasoned with salt, so that you may know how to answer everyone" (Col. 4:5–6).

People Need God

1

Before the D-Team Experience

LEADER DEVOTION

Take some time to read Matthew 5:43–48. As you prepare to lead this unit on evangelism, think about how these verses apply to your life. Do you have any enemies? This first lesson deals with the fact that everyone matters to God. This includes people whom we sometimes consider our enemies—the sick, the rapists, the homosexuals, the powerful, et cetera. Do you live your life condemning sinners or praying for them? Are you more concerned with hating than loving? Do you run away from these people or toward them? These verses remind us to pray for our enemies. Take a few moments to pray for your enemies, sinners, the depraved, and the sick. Then pray that you will reflect God's love to these people rather than point a condemning finger and turn away from them.

LOOKING AHEAD

Student Focus

Every D-Team member will discover the first urgent reason we are called to evangelize by studying two supporting truths:

Truth #1: God created everyone in His own image.
Truth #2: Everyone is lost without God.

Unit Memory Verse

"Be wise in the way you act toward outsiders; make the most of every opportunity. Let your conversation be always full of grace, seasoned with salt, so that you may know how to answer everyone" (Col. 4:5–6).

Practical Impact

By the end of this D-Team experience, your students will have developed a sense of urgency toward the lost people of this world. Each student will have the opportunity to pray for a lost soul and will be given a coin to take home with him or her as a reminder of the parable of the lost coin.

BE PREPARED

Materials Needed

- Bibles and pens
- Duplicated Student Notes
- Pictures or names of lost souls
- Envelopes
- One coin for each student

Special Preparation

Prepare your envelopes so that each contains a picture of a person and a coin inside for each D-Team member. Cut the pictures out of newspapers or magazines. Try to find dramatic pictures to symbolize lost souls.

Environment

To set up the environment for this D-Team experience, you can choose one of the following. Option 1 works in any setting; Option 2 moves the experience outside your normal setting.

Option 1: Demonstrate to your D-Team members the lost people of the world by painting a vivid picture of the void in people's lives. Bring in videotapes, photos, audio tapes, or statistics of starving people in third-world countries, drug-users, prostitutes, suicide victims, gang members, politicians, Hollywood stars, et cetera. Consider what will have the strongest impact on *your* D-Team members. For some, it might be more powerful to focus on homeless or indigenous people. Others might benefit more by examining the lives of people with immense wealth and power. Or you may want to look at both extremes and pose the question: "Who needs God more?" Have a brief discussion and make sure your students realize everyone needs God.

Option 2: Take your D-Team members to a place where they can see lost people firsthand. Consider what will leave the strongest impression. You might take them to a homeless shelter, walk down the streets of an inner-city neighborhood, or go to a mall, train station, or restaurant. Make sure your students realize that no matter what a person's sins or lifestyle, he or she matters to God.

Prep Notes

Leading the D-Team Experience

(60 min. total)

GET STARTED

(5 min.)

Unit Preview

Have a student read aloud the following information from the "Preview" in the Student Notes: ***As you work together through "Unit 1: Right Here, Right Now," you will discover three reasons why it is urgent for us to evangelize:***

1. ***People need God.***
2. ***We have the answer.***
3. ***Life is short.***

Unit Memory Verse

Read aloud Colossians 4:5–6, "Be wise in the way you act toward outsiders; make the most of every opportunity. Let your conversation be always full of grace, seasoned with salt, so that you may know how to answer everyone." Explain that Paul instructed the Colossian believers to make the most of every opportunity to speak to others about Christ.

Student Prayer

Have a student pray that there will be no distractions during this D-Team experience, and that each student will realize the urgency of this message.

Focus

Share with your D-Team members that this week every member will discover the first urgent reason we are called to evangelize: People need God. They will make this discovery by studying two supporting truths:

Truth #1: God created everyone in His own image.
Truth #2: Everyone is lost without God.

THE EXPERIENCE

(40 min.)

Begin this D-Team experience with a brief discussion about the fact that everyone needs God. Ask: ***What is the difference between need and want?*** Give them a few minutes to complete the list of needs and wants in their Student Notes. Point out that wants are usually temporary desires whereas needs have much more importance. Needs are usually necessary for survival. Explain that our relationship with God is a need not only for this life, but for life eternal as well.

Truth #1: God created everyone in His own image.
Have a student ***read aloud Colossians 1:16–17.*** Discuss the following questions from the Student Notes:
If you were to list the things God has created, what would you include?
Encourage students to include "things invisible" in their lists.
What does it mean that "all things hold together" in Christ?

Take some time to discuss the magnitude of this verse. You may want to make parallels to a mother and her new baby. Discuss the unbelievable bond and how both need each other. Ask your students to imagine how much more God must have these feelings toward us.

Prep Notes

Have the students pair up and look up the following verses. Instruct them to write a brief summary of each passage in their Student Notes.

Genesis 1:26—God made man in His image.
Job 1:21—God is sovereign in making choices and decisions that affect our lives.
1 John 3:2—We are children of God, and we will be like Him.
Matthew 6:8—God knows what we need before we ask Him.
Jeremiah 1:4—Before we were born, God knew everything about us.

After your students have looked up these verses, help them to see that these verses apply to every single person created by God. One way you might get them to realize this would be to display the pictures you collected for Option 1 at the opening of this experience. Or you might have your students list the groups of people they consider sinners (murderers, thieves, prostitutes, etc.). Remind the students that these verses apply to every group listed—and more. God created all of us in His image and desperately wants all of us to develop a relationship with Him. Imagine how a mother would feel if her child never even acknowledged her. God hates sin but loves the sinner. This is what we too must do if we want to be true evangelists.

Truth #2: Everyone is lost without God.
Have your students skim Luke 15. Remind them that, although God created us in His own image, we are all lost until we are willing to turn to Him. Tell your students that this is why evangelism is so urgent.

Divide your D-Team members into three drama teams. Instruct each team to act out or present one of the following parables from Luke 15: ***the lost sheep (vv. 3–7); the lost coin (vv. 8–10); the lost son (vv. 11–31).*** If you only have a few members, assign a parable to each individual and have him or her paraphrase it.

After each team or individual's presentation, discuss the following questions.

What is the significance of the first two verses in Luke 15? Note that these verses set the stage for what is to come. They demonstrate how we need to be willing to associate with the "sinners" as Jesus did if we want to see lost people saved. However, too often we are like the Pharisees and the teachers of the law.
How do you think it makes Jesus feels when someone wanders from the flock?
Have you ever lost something valuable? How did you feel? How did you feel when you found it?
How would you have responded to the lost son if you were his father? If you were his brother?

In summary, remind your students that there is an urgent reason for us to evangelize—people need God. We must remind ourselves that God created everyone in His own image and that everyone is lost without Him. Jesus explains in His parables just how important it is to seek out the lost. We must not sit back and wait for someone else to do it!

(5 min.)

REFLECTION

Give each D-Team member an envelope with a picture of a person and a coin inside. Ask your students to find a quiet place, open the envelope, and pray for the face or group of people that the picture represents. When your students have finished praying, instruct them to take a good look at the coin. Explain that the coin represents the lost of this world who need God. Encourage your D-Team members to take their coins home with them and place them where they will be reminded of the need to be constantly in search of "that which is lost."

Prep Notes

Give your students a few moments to record honest responses to the following questions found on their Student Notes: ***What was most meaningful to you about our experience today? What does God want you to do in response?***

Ask a student to read aloud the Summary Statements in the Student Notes.

Summary Statements

We learned today that . . .

- Our world is filled with lost souls living only for themselves and their personal gratification.
- If we are going to make a difference in this world we must remember that God created everyone—even the most wretched of sinners.
- When we remember that God loves everyone who is lost, we will be more determined to devote ourselves fully to reaching out to the lost of the world.

MAKE AN IMPACT

(10 min.)

. . . In Your Life

Ask your D-Team members to make a contact list of places and names of people they meet during the next week who are "lost." As they go through the week, encourage them to write down the place (school, work, home, etc.) and the name (or description) of every person they come across who appears to be lost.

. . . With Accountability

Have your D-Team members form pairs to become accountability partners for the week and to work on the memory verse. Have each student begin learning the **Unit Memory Verse** by writing it out in the space provided in the Student Notes.

Prayer

Bring the students back together and close in prayer.

MAKE AN IMPACT

. . . In Your Life
Make a contact list of places and names of people you meet during the next week who are lost. As you go through the week, write down the place (school, work, home, etc.) and the name (or description) of every person you come across who appears to be lost.

. . . With Accountability
With your accountability partner, talk about your responses to the "Reflection" questions. Exchange phone numbers. Call each other this week to hold each other accountable to making an impact in your life.

name	phone

Begin learning your memory verse by writing it out in the space below.

MEMORY VERSE

Colossians 4:5–6

1. People Need God

Preview
As you work together through "Unit 1: Right Here, Right Now," you will discover three reasons why it is urgent for us to evangelize:

1. People need God.
2. We have the answer.
3. Life is short.

Unit Memory Verse
"Be wise in the way you act toward outsiders; make the most of every opportunity. Let your conversation be always full of grace, seasoned with salt, so that you may know how to answer everyone" (Col. 4:5–6).

Focus
This week, you will discover the first urgent reason we are called to evangelize: People need God. You will make this discovery by studying two supporting truths.

THE EXPERIENCE

What is the difference between need and want?

Make a list of the wants and the needs in your life.

The needs in my life are:

The wants in my life are:

Truth #1: God created everyone in His own image.
Read Colossians 1:16–17. If you were to list the things God has created, what would you include?

What does it mean that "all things hold together" in Christ?

Read each of the following verses and write a brief summary of each passage.

Genesis 1:26

Job 1:21

1 John 3:2

Matthew 6:8

Jeremiah 1:4

Truth #2: Everyone is lost without God.
Skim Luke 15. Read your assigned parable and be prepared to act it out or paraphrase it. Make notes in the space below.

The lost sheep (vv. 3–7)

The lost coin (vv. 8–10)

The lost son (vv. 11–31)

What is the significance of the first two verses in Luke 15?

How do you think it makes Jesus feel when someone wanders from the flock?

Have you ever lost something valuable? How did you feel? How did you feel when you found it?

How would you have responded to the lost son if you were his father? If you were his brother?

REFLECTION

You will receive an envelope with a picture of a person and a coin inside. Find a quiet place, open the envelope, and pray for the face or group of people that the picture represents. When you have finished praying, take a good look at the coin. It represents the lost people of this world who need God. Take your coin home with you and place it where you will be reminded of the need to be constantly in search of "that which is lost."

What was most meaningful to you about our experience today?

What does God want you to do in response?

Summary Statements

We learned today that . . .

- Our world is filled with lost souls living only for themselves and their personal gratification.
- If we are going to make a difference in this world we must remember that God created everyone—even the most wretched of sinners.
- When we remember that God loves everyone who is lost, we will be more determined to devote ourselves fully to reaching out the lost of the world.

We Have the Answer

2

Before the D-Team Experience

LEADER DEVOTION

Before you lead this D-Team experience, spend some time reflecting on your role as a leader. Are you committed to your students? Do you pray for them daily? Do you go out of your way to get involved in their lives? Is *your* life in balance? Are you consistent with your quiet time? Are you constantly seeking ways to evangelize your friends? Are you a leader for the right reasons? Think through these questions. Be honest with yourself and God. Pray right now for help in these areas. If you are in contact with other leaders in your ministry, make it a point this week to ask them how they are doing and where they could use prayer. Make a difference in your ministry!

LOOKING AHEAD

Student Focus
Every D-Team member will discover that the second urgent reason we are called to evangelize is because we have the answer. They will make this discovery by doing two things:

Action Step #1: *Know* that we have the only answer.
Action Step #2: *Tell* the answer to everyone.

Unit Memory Verse
"Be wise in the way you act toward outsiders; make the most of every opportunity. Let your conversation be always full of grace, seasoned with salt, so that you may know how to answer everyone" (Col. 4:5–6).

Practical Impact
By the end of this D-Team experience, your students will realize they have the answer for this world, and it is urgent they not delay in telling it. They will be given a "pill" as a reminder that they have the "cure" for a sick world, and it must not be kept hidden from the rest of the world.

BE PREPARED

Materials Needed

- Bibles and pens
- Duplicated Student Notes
- M&Ms or some sort of candy that looks like a pill
- Envelopes (one for each student)

Special Preparation

- Videotape a short clip from the TV show *E.R.* (Option 1).
- Research and be prepared to report on some statistics about AIDS, heart

attacks, cancer, and other life-threatening, incurable medical problems (Option 1).

- Enclose an M&M (or some sort of candy that looks like a pill) in an envelope for each D-Team member.

Environment

To set up the environment for this D-Team experience, you can choose one of the following. Option 1 works in any setting; Option 2 moves the experience outside your normal setting.

Option 1: This D-Team experience deals with the idea that we have a cure for the sick and lost of this world. Begin with a clip from the TV show *E.R.* Or share some statistics about AIDS, heart attacks, cancer, and other life-threatening, incurable medical problems. If you have access to medical equipment or clothing, you might want to dress up like a doctor or wear a stethoscope around your neck. Get your students into the mind-set that illness is everywhere. Explain that we spend billions of dollars each year trying to come up with medical solutions.

Option 2: Take your D-Team members to a hospital waiting room or medical facility. If you or your students know any doctors or nurses, you might ask them to come to the beginning of your D-Team meeting to discuss the world's illnesses. If you have students who have experienced family or personal medical tragedies, ask them if they would be willing to share their experience with the group.

Prep Notes

Leading the D-Team Experience

(60 min. total)

GET STARTED

(5 min.)

Review
Have a student read aloud the information under "Review" in the Student Notes: ***Last week we discovered that people need God. This week we will discover that we have the answer that must be told.***

Student Prayer
Have each student in your group pray for an understanding of how he or she can participate in the "cure" for the world.

Focus
Share with your group that during this D-Team experience they will discover the second urgent reason we are called to evangelize: We have the answer. They will make this discovery by doing two things:

Action Step #1: ***Know*** **that we have the only answer.**
Action Step #2: ***Tell*** **the answer to everyone.**

THE EXPERIENCE

(40 min.)

After a brief discussion about the medical world in Option 1 or Option 2, ask your students: ***If you had the cure to the AIDS virus, would you share it? Why?*** Be sensitive to students in your group who might be currently involved in medical tragedies.

Have a student ***read aloud Matthew 9:12.*** Ask your students: ***How does this verse apply to us?*** Help them realize that we must not surround ourselves only with believers. Note that last week we learned that we must reach out to the world because everyone is lost without Christ.

Action Step #1: ***Know*** **that we have the only answer.**
Have a student ***read aloud 1 Corinthians 15:1–2.*** Explain that the Corinthians to whom Paul wrote were considered "least likely to convert" to the Christian faith. They were highly immoral and involved in cults and whatever would lead to a "good time." In chapter 15, Paul reminds us of the basis of Christianity.

Have your students discuss the following questions in their Student Notes:

How do these verses remind us of the Gospel? (They remind us that our faith is based on the truth that Christ died for our sins.)

Do you still believe this is the way to be healed from sin? Why or why not? (Explain that this is the only way to be healed.)

Use the last question as the springboard for a discussion about why Christ's death and resurrection is the only cure for sin. Use medical analogies to make the picture clear. Here are some comparisons you might make:

Prep Notes

- There are people in this world who are "sick" and desperately seeking the "right" cure.
- There are no choices in treatments, no value in getting a second opinion. The Bible is very clear that there is only one way to be cured.
- If we truly believe we have been healed, we should be anxious to tell every single person we meet.

Ask a student to ***read aloud 1 John 1:1–4.*** Have your students discuss the following questions in their Student Notes:

What is the author of these verses anxious to proclaim? (He wants to share his discovery that eternal life is found through Christ.)

According to verse 4, why was this written? (To make our joy complete.)
How might sharing this news with others make our joy complete?

Action Step #2: *Tell* the answer to everyone.
Remind your students that when we think about sharing this cure that we have, we must not present it as if we are all-knowing, powerful doctors and everyone else is just a poor, helpless weakling. We must remember that we are sick people telling other sick people where to get healed. We are going to take a look at how Jesus was willing to tell everyone with whom He came into contact. Notice that He didn't spend all His time talking with those who were already healed!

Have your D-Team members study the following stories about Jesus sharing the Good News. You may read them aloud as a group, paraphrase them, or you might divide the group and have the students tell the stories. After each story is presented, have your students determine *whom* Jesus told, *how* He told the person, and *why* He told the person.

Jesus meets two men on the road (Matt. 20:29–34)
Who—Two blind men sitting by the roadside in Jericho
How—Jesus responded to their shouts, asked them what they wanted from Him, and healed them.
Why—Because He had compassion on them, Jesus healed them and they followed Him.

Jesus visits a tax collector (Luke 19:1–10)
Who—Zacchaeus, a short, wealthy tax collector
How—Jesus called to him and invited Himself to dinner.
Why—Even though the crowd was upset that Jesus would associate with this man, Jesus wanted every soul to be saved.

Jesus at Jacob's well (John 4:1–26)
Who—a Samaritan woman who was an adulteress
How—Through His actions and His analogy of the water of eternal life.
Why—Although Jews did not usually associate with Samaritans, Jesus looked at this woman as a sick and hurting soul who needed salvation—not as an enemy.

After reading these stories about how effectively Jesus was able to tell even the outcasts of society, explain that there is a lot of room for improvement in our own lives. Remind your students that although we can't use miracles to back up what we have to say, we can still follow Jesus' example by reaching out to everyone (including those who appear to be incurable), and by being straightforward with our words.

Say: ***Jesus didn't just add people to His kingdom; He multiplied the numbers.***
Ask: ***What does this statement mean? How can it be applied in our lives?*** Point

Prep Notes

out that Jesus didn't just tell individuals in secret; he witnessed in crowds. And when people accepted His message, *they* were told how to spread the Good News. It's like the shampoo commercial—and they told two friends, and they told two friends, and so on and so on and so on. This is how evangelism should work!

REFLECTION

(5 min.)

Give each D-Team member an envelope with an M&M enclosed. Ask your students, "If you knew this one pill could solve every illness, every problem in the world, and there was an endless supply, what would you do with it?" (Obviously they would share it with as many people as possible.) Have your students take a few minutes to think about who in their life needs this pill most right now. Tell them that this pill represents the answer we hold within our hearts. Have them spend some time in prayer for this person. Then tell them to take the pill home as a reminder of the cure we all have within us.

Give your students a few moments to record honest responses to the following questions found in their Student Notes: ***What was most meaningful to you about our experience today? What does God want you to do in response?***

Ask a student to read aloud the Summary Statements in the Student Notes.

Summary Statements

We learned today that . . .

- The world around us is sick.
- We have accepted the fact that Christ died to save us.
- We know this is the only answer.
- We must tell this cure to the world.
- We have the answer within us, so why wouldn't we share it?

MAKE AN IMPACT

(10 min.)

. . . In Your Life

Have your students review the list of contacts they made last week. Encourage them to select one name from their list and commit themselves to giving that person a "pill" this week. Challenge your D-Team members to spend time praying for the right opportunity and for the Holy Spirit to work in the life of that person. If some of your students did not make a contact list last week, have them select one person in their lives who needs to hear the answer they have.

. . . With Accountability

Have the D-Team members form pairs to become accountability partners for the week and to work on the memory verse. Have each student write out the **Unit Memory Verse**.

Prayer

Bring the students back together and close in prayer.

Summary Statements

We learned today that . . .

- The world around us is sick.
- We have accepted the fact that Christ died to save us.
- We know that this is the only answer.
- We must tell this cure to the world.
- We have the answer within us, so why wouldn't we share it?

MAKE AN IMPACT

. . . In Your Life
Review the list of contacts you made last week. Select one name from your list and commit to giving that person a "pill" this week. Don't forget that you don't necessarily have to give the whole dose at once. Some cures are a gradual process. Spend some time praying for the right opportunity and for the Holy Spirit to work in the life of that person. If you did not make a contact list last week, select one person in your life who needs to hear the answer you have.

. . . With Accountability
With your accountability partner, talk about your responses to the "Reflection" questions. Exchange phone numbers. Call each other this week to hold each other accountable to making an impact in your life.

name	phone

Review your memory verse by writing it out in the space below. Then recite it to your partner.

MEMORY VERSE
Colossians 4:5–6

2. We Have the Answer

Preview
Last week we discovered that people need God. This week we will discover that we have the answer that must be told.

Focus
Today you will discover the second urgent reason we are called to evangelize is because we have the answer. You will make this discovery by doing two things.

THE EXPERIENCE

If you had the cure to the AIDS virus, would you share it? Why?

Read aloud Matthew 9:12. How does this verse apply to us?

Action Step #1: *Know* that we have the only answer.
Read aloud 1 Corinthians 15:1–4. Then answer the following questions:

How do these verses remind us of the Gospel?

Do you still believe that this is the way to be healed from sin? Why or why not?

Read aloud 1 John 1:1–4. Then answer the following questions:

What is the author of these verses anxious to proclaim?

According to verse 4, why was this written?

How might sharing this news with others make our joy complete?

Action Step #2: *Tell* the answer to everyone.
Study the following stories about Jesus sharing the Good News. After each story is presented, students determine *whom* Jesus told, *how* He told the person, and *why* He told the person.

Jesus meets two men on the road (Matt. 20:29–34)
Who—

How—

Why—

Jesus visits a tax collector (Luke 19:1–10)
Who—

How—

Why—

Jesus at Jacob's well (John 4:1–26)
Who—

How—

Why—

Jesus didn't just add people to His kingdom; He multiplied the numbers. What does this statement mean? How can it be applied in our lives?

REFLECTION

You will be given an envelope with an M&M enclosed. If you knew this one pill could solve every illness, every problem in the world, and there was an endless supply, what would you do with it?

Take a few minutes to think about who in your life needs this pill most right now. Spend some time in prayer for this person. Then take the pill home as a reminder of the cure we all have within us.

What was most meaningful to you about our experience today?

What does God want you to do in response?

3

Life Is Short

Before the D-Team Experience

LEADER DEVOTION

Take some time to read Romans 8:28–38. These verses remind us that we are conquerors, and that nothing can separate us from the love of God. Notice that we are never promised that nothing bad will ever happen to us; rather, we have the guarantee that God will use those bad things for our good. Do you believe this? Are you living this in your life? Pray that even during the trying times you will not becme frustrated or doubtful, but will instead grow stronger.

LOOKING AHEAD

Student Focus
Every D-Team member will discover that the third urgent reason we are called to evangelize is because life is short. They will make this discovery as they identify and believe the following facts:

Fact #1: Time does not stop.
Fact #2: Everyone dies.
Fact #3: People will spend eternity in heaven or hell.
Fact #4: There are people we may only see once in our lives.
Fact #5: The time is now!

Unit Memory Verse
"Be wise in the way you act toward outsiders; make the most of every opportunity. Let your conversation be always full of grace, seasoned with salt, so that you may know how to answer everyone" (Col. 4:5–6).

Practical Impact
By the end of this D-Team experience, your students will realize that life is short, and it is imperative that they not delay in telling their friends about Jesus. Students will make some calculations regarding how well they are using their time on earth.

BE PREPARED

Materials Needed
- Bibles and pens
- Duplicated Student Notes
- A piece of paper for each student
- A calculator for each student

Environment
To set up the environment for this D-Team experience, you can choose one of the following. Option 1 works in any setting; Option 2 moves the experience outside your normal setting.

Option 1: This D-Team experience deals with the urgency of evangelism. You will be helping your students realize how quickly life goes by, and that our stay on earth is only temporary. Have your students share a childhood memory. After each student has done this, have them think for a moment about how fast life has passed by from that day to this. Ask them to think about how much of their lives they have spent sleeping, eating, going to school, etc. Then ask them to consider how much of their lives they have spent telling others about Christ. Or you might want to get your students to think about death and how quickly and unexpectedly it comes. Ask a student to share a personal story. You could also get into a discussion about what students are fearful of, and what they are looking forward to, in terms of death. Be sensitive to students who might be grieving or who are uncomfortable with the topic.

Option 2: Take your students to a graveyard or cemetery. Encourage the students to wander through the cemetery. Tell them to meet back at a certain spot in five minutes. Debrief by asking them if they were scared, sad, or unaffected. Help them realize that life is short and that none of us know when our time on this earth will be finished. Point out that our life on earth is only a temporary stop on our way to an eternal home. Ask them if they have any friends who would not go to heaven if they were to die today.

Leading the D-Team Experience

(60 min. total)

Prep Notes

GET STARTED

(5 min.)

Review

Have a student read aloud the following information from the "Review" section in the Student Notes: ***Two weeks ago we discovered that people need God. Last week we discovered that we have the answer that must be told. This week we will learn that life is short and we must take ownership of sharing the answer with others.***

Student Prayer

Have a student in your group pray for the lost people of the world.

Focus

Share with your group that during this D-Team experience they will discover the third urgent reason we are called to evangelize: Life is short. They will make this discovery as they identify and believe the following facts:

Fact #1: Time does not stop.
Fact #2: Everyone dies.
Fact #3: People will spend eternity in heaven or hell.
Fact #4: There are people we may only see once in our lives.
Fact #5: The time is now!

THE EXPERIENCE

(40 min.)

Fact #1: Time does not stop.

Ask a student what time it is. As soon as the person gives you the time, say, "Do you realize that you can never give someone the exact time because time is constantly changing?" Have a brief discussion about time. Some of the questions you might want to ask are: "Why do we have time? Do we need time? Do you wish time moved faster or slower? What would the world be like without time? Does time even exist?" Try to get your students to realize that time is just a measurement humans have made up to calculate our stay on earth. It is important in terms of our communication with each other, but in the "big picture," it doesn't really matter because this life is only temporary. Time is a gift from God.

Ask two students to read aloud the following passages: ***1 Chronicles 29:15 and Job 8:9.*** Then discuss the following questions.
What does it mean that "our days on earth are but a shadow"? (Our lives here on earth are temporary.)
If our days on earth are just a shadow, why are we even here? (To glorify God and enhance His kingdom.)

Fact #2: Everyone dies.

Ask: ***Would you rather know the day you are going to die, or would you rather it was a surprise? Why?*** Point out that the fact is all of us will die. The question is when and how much will we accomplish before that time. Divide the following verses among your students:
Genesis 3:19 (We started as dust, and we will eventually return to dust.)

Prep Notes

Job 7:9 (No one can avoid death. No one can save himself from the grave.)
Psalm 89:48 (As clouds vanish and are gone, so too is human life transitory.)

Have each write a brief summary of the assigned verse. When everyone has completed the assignment, go around the room and have students summarize their verses.

Explain that all of the verses deal with the fact that everyone will die. Say, "Now that we realize our time on earth is short and that everyone will die, what happens to us after we die?"

Fact #3: People will spend eternity in heaven or hell.
Have your students close their eyes. Ask them to imagine what heaven will be like. Now have them open their eyes and jot down some ideas in their Student Notes. They may share these with everyone. Now have them do the same thing with hell. Remind them that we have already discussed that everyone dies and will end up in one of these places.

Have half of your students read the verses about heaven listed in the Student notes and work together to create a picture of what they think heaven will be like. (They can either sketch an actual picture in their Student Notes or jot down a word picture.) Assign the other students the verses about hell and have them create a picture of it. (If your time is short, you can eliminate some of the verses from either list.)

heaven	***hell***
Matthew 13:44	***Psalm 73:27***
John 3:18	***Matthew 13:49***
John 5:29	***Luke 12:5***
John 14:2–4	***Luke 13:3***
Revelation 20:15	***John 3:18***
	John 5:29

Have each group share their picture with the other group.

Fact #4: There are people we may only see once in our lives.
Have each student spend some quiet time on his or her own answering the following questions:
If you died today, would you go to heaven or hell? How do you know?

Do you have any close friends who would go to hell if they died today?

Have you shared the answer of the Good News with these friends? Why or why not?

Think about people with whom you come in contact every day (teachers, relatives, co-workers, someone in your school, etc.). If you knew that tomorrow was the last day you would ever see this person, what would you say to him or her? What is holding you back?

Fact #5: The time is now!
So far, your students have uncovered several important truths about life: time goes fast; everyone dies; everyone will spend eternity in heaven or hell; there are people in our lives whom we may only see once. Note that the most important truth they can learn today is that the time is now!

The following verses all deal with the idea that we don't have much time and it is up to us to spread the truth as soon as possible. ***Read aloud Matthew 24:44 and Luke 12:40.*** Ask: ***What key words do these two verses have in common?*** ("Be ready.")

Why is it important for us as evangelists to realize that Christ could come at any time? (We must not delay in telling our friends. We can't wait for the "right moment." *Now* is the time.) ***What is preventing you from spreading the Gospel to everyone with whom you come into contact?***

Prep Notes

REFLECTION

(5 min.)

Hand out a piece of paper and a calculator to each student. Then ask your D-Team members to estimate the number of hours a day they spend sleeping, eating, watching TV, in school, talking on the phone, in the car, and hanging out with friends.

When your D-Team members have finished, have them add the total number of hours spent in these activities and then multiply the total by 365. They should then take this answer and multiply it by 5 years less than their age. For example, if a student is 15, he or she will be multiplying the answer by 10. Announce that this final total is the number of nonproductive or empty hours they have squandered since they were 5 years old! Be sure that your students understand you are simply demonstrating how many hours pass without us even realizing it. We must realize that God gives time to us as a gift, and we must use our time wisely by giving it back to Him and building His Kingdom.

Give your students a few moments to record honest responses to the following questions found in their Student Notes: ***What was most meaningful to you about our experience today? What does God want you to do in response?***

Ask a student to read aloud the Summary Statements in the Student Notes.

Summary Statements

We learned today that . . .

- Time does not stop.
- Everyone dies.
- People will spend eternity in heaven or hell.
- There are people we may only see once in our lives.
- The time is now!

MAKE AN IMPACT

(10 min.)

. . . In Your Life

Ask your students if they are using their time for Christ or for themselves. Encourage your students to keep a mini-journal during the next week. On the top of each page they should write Day 1, Day 2, etc. Each night they should take a few moments to reflect on their day. Challenge them to write down how much time was spent that day living for themselves, and how much time was spent building God's kingdom. They should also record every time they took a step closer to bringing someone to Christ.

. . . With Accountability

Have the D-Team members form pairs to become accountability partners for the week and to work on the memory verse. Have each student write out the **Unit Memory Verse**, recite it to his or her partner, and share a way the verse is meaningful in his or her life.

Prayer

Bring the students back together and close in prayer.

Summary Statements

We learned today that . . .
- Time does not stop.
- Everyone dies.
- People will spend eternity in heaven or hell.
- There are people we may only see once in our lives.
- The time is now!

. . . In Your Life
Are you using your time for Christ or for yourself? Keep a mini-journal during the next week. On the top of each page, write Day 1, Day 2, etc. Each night, take a few moments to reflect on your day. Write down how much time was spent that day living for yourself, and how much time was spent building God's kingdom. You should also record every time you took a step closer to bringing someone to Christ.

. . . With Accountability
With your accountability partner, talk about your responses to the "Reflection" questions. Exchange phone numbers. Call each other this week to hold each other accountable to making an impact in your life.

name	phone

Review your memory verse by writing it out in the space below. After reciting it to your partner, share a way the verse is meaningful in your life.

MEMORY VERSE
Colossians 4:5–6

3. Life Is Short

Review
Two weeks ago we discovered that people need God. Last week we discovered that we have the answer that must be told. This week we will learn that life is short and we must take ownership of sharing the answer with others.

Focus
You will discover the third urgent reason we are called to evangelize: Life is short. You will make this discovery as you identify and believe five facts.

Fact #1: Time does not stop.
Read 1 Chronicles 29:15 and Job 8:9.

What does it mean that "our days on earth are but a shadow"?

If our days on earth are just a shadow, why are we even here?

Fact #2: Everyone dies.
Would you rather know the day you are going to die, or would you rather it was a surprise? Why?

Read your assigned verses and be prepared to share a brief summary.

Genesis 3:19

Job 7:9

Psalm 89:48

Fact #3: People will spend eternity in heaven or hell.
Read the following verses:

heaven	*hell*
Matthew 13:44	Psalm 73:27
John 3:18	Matthew 13:49
John 5:29	Luke 12:5
John 14:2–4	Luke 13:3
Revelation 20:15	John 3:18
	John 5:29

Fact #4: There are people we may only see once in our lives.
Spend some quiet time on your own answering the following questions:

If you died today, would you go to heaven or hell? How do you know?

Do you have any close friends who would go to hell if they died today?

Have you shared the answer of the Good News with these friends? Why or why not?

Think about people with whom you come in contact every day (teachers, relatives, co-workers, someone in your school, etc.). If you knew that tomorrow was the last day you would ever see this person, what would you say to him or her? What is holding you back?

Fact #5: The time is now!
Read Matthew 24:44 and Luke 12:40.
What key words do these two verses have in common?

Why is it important for us as evangelists to realize that Christ could come at any time?

What is preventing you from spreading the Gospel to everyone with whom you come into contact?

REFLECTION

Using the paper and calculator you receive, determine how many hours a day you spend:

Sleeping—

Eating—

Watching TV—

In school—

Talking on the phone—

In the car—

Hanging out with friends—

Now add the total number of hours spent in these activities and then multiply the total by 365. Take this answer and multiply it by 5 years less than your age. For example, if you are 15, you will be multiplying the answer by 10. This final total is the number of nonproductive or empty hours you have squandered since you were 5 years old.

What was most meaningful to you about our experience today?

What does God want you to do in response?

FISHING FOR FRIENDS

STUDENT IMPACT

Unit 2 Introduction

LEADER FOCUS

Read Matthew 9:36–38. Read it again. What is the Holy Spirit saying to you through these words? How do these verses apply to the students in your ministry? How do the verses apply to those students in your community who don't know Jesus personally? Do you see them the way Jesus does? Take a moment to reflect on your answers to these questions before diving into this unit of D-Team experiences.

BIG PICTURE

Unit Overview
In Unit 2 you will be focusing on accomplishing one goal—teaching your students how to evangelize. Every D-Team member will learn how to evangelize by answering three crucial questions: (1) *What do you believe?* (2) *What should you say?* (3) *What is the power source?*

1. Fishing Tackle
During this D-Team experience, your students will answer the question, *What do you believe?* by understanding and affirming five statements of faith:

Faith Statement #1: I believe I am a sinner.
Faith Statement #2: I believe the penalty for my sin is death.
Faith Statement #3: I believe God sent His Son, Jesus, to die for my sins.
Faith Statement #4: I believe Jesus conquered death, which was the penalty for my sins, by rising from the dead.
Faith Statement #5: I believe if I confess and believe with my heart the first four statements, then I will be saved.

2. Fishing Stories
During this D-Team experience, your students will answer the question, *What should I say?* by preparing to share their faith as they work through a three step plan:

Step #1: Write out your story.
Step #2: Integrate Scripture into your story.
Step #3: Share your story with others.

3. Fishing Fuel
During this D-Team experience, your students will answer the question, *What is the power source?* by answering two life-changing questions:

Unit 2 Introduction

Question #1: What is the true power source?
Question #2: How do we tap into it?

Unit Memory Verse
"I am not ashamed of the Gospel, because it is the power of God for the salvation of everyone who believes: first for the Jew, then for the Gentile" (Rom. 1:16).

Fishing Tackle

1

Before the D-Team Experience

LEADER DEVOTION

What do you believe? Strip everything away, and what is at the core of your faith? What would you defend without a doubt? What would you die for because you know it to be unchangeable truth?

We live in a society that changes at such an incredibly fast pace that it leaves us spinning. Just when we start to understand the rules to the game of life, someone makes an adjustment that rocks our world. We have a deep need for something stable. Unchanging. Something we can stand on. Live by. Die with, knowing it will not change. This D-Team experience will bring us back to the basic truths that introduced us into an intimate relationship with the Creator of the world. Take your time preparing for this session. Enjoy the refreshment of promises and truths that will never change. Don't miss the opportunity to worship Jesus.

LOOKING AHEAD

Student Focus

Every D-Team member will answer the question, "What do you believe?" by understanding and affirming five statements of faith:

Faith Statement #1: I believe I am a sinner.
Faith Statement #2: I believe the penalty for my sin is death.
Faith Statement #3: I believe God sent His Son, Jesus, to die for my sins.
Faith Statement #4: I believe Jesus conquered death, which was the penalty for my sins, by rising from the dead.
Faith Statement #5: I believe if I confess and believe with my heart the first four statements, then I will be saved.

Unit Memory Verse

"I am not ashamed of the Gospel, because it is the power of God for the salvation of everyone who believes: first for the Jew, then for the Gentile" (Rom. 1:16).

Practical Impact

During this D-Team experience, you will be helping your students put into words what they believe about their faith. In order to illustrate those five faith statements, bring five different pieces of fishing tackle that are a must for fishing—one for each statement. Get yourself educated on how to use them so you can explain them to your students!

BE PREPARED

Materials Needed

- Bibles and pens
- Duplicated Student Notes

- Fishing rods (one for each student)
- Fishing tackle: line, weights, hooks, bobber, lures, bait, leaders, swivels, etc.
- Fishing video, VCR, TV (Option 1)

Special Preparation

- Borrow fishing rods (one for each student) from church members, or ask students to bring one to this D-Team experience.
- Familiarize yourself with the various kinds of fishing tackle.

Environment

To set up the environment for this D-Team experience, you can choose one of the following. Option 1 works in any setting; Option 2 moves the experience outside your normal setting.

Option 1: As students gather, show a clip of a video that depicts fishing such as an educational film, fishing TV show, or the movie *A River Runs Through It.*

Option 2: Meet by a small lake, stream, or pond. You could also meet in a boat or out on a small dock. Don't use any location that will cause distractions or put people in possible danger.

Prep Notes

Leading the D-Team Experience

(60 min. total)

GET STARTED

(5 min.)

Unit Preview

Have a student read aloud the following information from the "Preview" in the Student Notes: ***As you work together through "Unit 2: Fishing for Friends," you will learn how to evangelize by answering three crucial questions: "What do you believe?" "What should you say?" and "What is the power source?"***

Unit Memory Verse

Read aloud Romans 1:16: "I am not ashamed of the Gospel, because it is the power of God for the salvation of everyone who believes: first for the Jew, then for the Gentile." Point out that the Gospel began with the Jews, who in turn were responsible for carrying that Gospel to other nations.

Student Prayer

Ask an upperclassman to pray for a clear understanding of the basics of the faith.

Focus

Share with your D-Team members that this week every member will answer the question, "What do you believe?" by understanding and affirming five statements of faith.

Faith Statement #1: I believe I am a sinner.
Faith Statement #2: I believe the penalty for my sin is death.
Faith Statement #3: I believe God sent His Son, Jesus, to die for my sins.
Faith Statement #4: I believe Jesus conquered death, which was the penalty for my sins, by rising from the dead.
Faith Statement #5: I believe if I confess and believe with my heart the first four statements, then I will be saved.

THE EXPERIENCE

(40 min.)

Begin your D-Team experience by ***reading aloud Luke 5:1–11.*** Explain that in this passage, the disciples were fishing in the Lake of Gennesaret when Jesus asked them to take Him out on water to preach. He went on to help them catch a boat load—literally—of fish. The disciples realized that this was no ordinary man, so they fell down at his feet. Jesus invited them to leave their trade of netting fish for a career in fishing for men. Ask: ***What did the disciples need in order to catch men? What do we need to "catch" our friends?***

Distribute the fishing poles and explain that you will be referring to them during this week and the next two D-Team experiences. Explain that the fishing pole represents our personal relationship to Jesus Christ. God is calling us to be fishers of our friends. What do we need to catch them? Point out that we will answer that question today as we examine five faith statements.

Faith Statement #1: I believe I am a sinner.

Remind the group that the first basic piece of fishing tackle vital for fishing success is the line. Take out the fishing rod, show your students where the line is, and explain the reason why you need a line to fish. Without it, the rod is pretty useless.

Tell your students that the first basic truth that is vital to believe in order to be a fisher of friends is found in Romans. Have a student ***read aloud Romans 3:10.*** Then have a student ***read aloud Romans 3:23.*** Ask: ***What do these verses indicate about our spiritual condition?*** (We are all sinners.)

Ask your students if they have any questions about this truth. If not, then ask them if they believe the truth they just looked at. If they can say yes confidently, then have them write, "I believe I am a sinner" in their Student Notes. If it is appropriate for your group, go around and have them say it out loud.

Faith Statement #2: I believe the penalty for my sin is death.
The second basic piece of fishing tackle that is vital for fishing success is the reel. Show your D-Team members where the reel is located on the fishing rod and explain why you need it to fish. Without it, we would not be able to pull the fish in once we caught it.

Tell the group that the second basic truth vital to being a fisher of friends is also found in Romans. Ask a student to ***read aloud Romans 6:23a.*** Ask: ***What does this verse tell us about sin?*** (The penalty for sin is death.)

Ask your students if they have any questions. If they can honestly agree with Romans 6:23a, then they should write, "I believe the penalty for my sin is death" in their Student Notes. If it is appropriate, go around again and quote the second faith statement out loud.

Faith Statement #3: I believe God sent His Son, Jesus, to die for my sins.
The third basic piece of fishing tackle vital for fishing success is a weight. Show your students where the weights should be placed and explain the reason why you need them to fish. Without them the line will not land where you want it to when you cast it—it is too light.

Tell the group that the third basic truth that is vital to believe in order to be a fisher of friends is found in ***Romans 5:6–8.*** Ask a student to read it aloud. Ask: ***What did God send Jesus to do for us?*** (Jesus died for our sins, because He loves us.)

Tell your group that they must now decide if they believe God sent His Son Jesus to die for their sins. If your students agree with this belief, have them write, "I believe God sent his Son, Jesus, to die for my sins" in their Student Notes. Then encourage them to say it aloud in unison.

Faith Statement #4: I believe Jesus conquered death, which was the penalty for my sins, by rising from the dead.
The fourth basic piece of fishing tackle vital for fishing success is the hook. Show your D-Team members where the hook should be placed and explain why you need it to catch fish. Without it, the attempt to catch anything would be futile!

Tell your group that the fourth basic truth that is vital to believe in order to be a fisher of friends is found in ***1 Corinthians 15:3–5.*** Ask a D-Team member to read it aloud. Then ask: ***In verse 4, what did Jesus do that was miraculous?*** (Jesus arose from the dead! No one else has ever done that!)

This one will challenge their faith. Are there any questions about it? Do your students really believe this? Ask them. If they agree with this truth, have them write, "I believe Jesus conquered death, which was the penalty for my sins, by rising from the dead"

Prep Notes

in their Student Notes. Again, if it is appropriate, have them go around and say it out loud.

Faith Statement #5: I believe if I confess and believe with my heart the first four statements, then I will be saved.
The fifth basic piece of fishing tackle vital for fishing success is the bait. Show your students where the bait should be placed and how to put it on. Explain that the reason why you need it is to persuade the fish to swallow the hook.

Tell your group that the fifth basic truth that is vital to believe in order to be a fisher of friends is found in ***Romans 10:9–10 and Ephesians 2:8–9.*** Ask a student to read each of these passages aloud. Then ask: ***According to these verses, what do we need to do in order to be saved?*** (We are to confess our faith and believe that God raised Jesus from the dead.)

If your students are able to agree that they believe each of the first four statements, then they are either Christians or they could potentially be ready to become followers by admitting they believe this last faith statement. This part of the D-Team could be an exciting opportunity for you as a leader to either affirm your students' faith in Jesus Christ or have an opportunity to lead a D-Team member to Christ. Ask your students if they can say they believe these truths with their whole heart. Then celebrate all the students—those who reaffirmed their faith, those who accepted Christ in your group, and those who are still seeking and investigating.

REFLECTION

(5 min.)

Today your D-Team members agreed with five statements of faith that are the basis for their relationship with Jesus. The following steps will help them when they are sharing their faith with their friends. Have your students open their Bibles and take the following steps:

Step 1: Turn to Romans 3:10. Highlight this verse and then write in the margin next to it "Romans 3:23."
Step 2: Turn to Romans 3:23. Highlight this verse and then write in the margin next to it "Romans 6:23."
Step 3: Turn to Romans 6:23. Highlight this verse and then write in the margin next to it "Romans 5:6–8."
Step 4: Turn to Romans 5:6–8. Highlight this verse and then write in the margin next to it "1 Corinthians 15:3–5."
Step 5: Turn to 1 Corinthians 15:3–5. Highlight this verse and then write in the margin next to it "Romans 10:9–10."
Step 6: Turn to Romans 10:9–10. Highlight this verse and then write in the margin next to it "Ephesians 2:8–9."
Step 7: Turn to Ephesians 2:8–9. Highlight this verse.

Point out that the only passage they have to remember is Romans 3:10 to begin to explain their faith to their friends.

Give your students a few moments to record honest responses to the following questions found in their Student Notes: ***What was most meaningful to you about our experience today? What does God want you to do in response?***

Ask a student to read aloud the Summary Statements in the Student Notes.

Prep Notes

Summary Statements

We learned today that . . .
- Five faith statements build the foundation for my faith.
- When sharing my faith with my friends, I can begin with Romans 3:10.

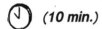

(10 min.)

MAKE AN IMPACT

. . . In Your Life
Ask your students to sit down with another believer this week and walk the person through the steps they recorded in their Bibles (Reflection). Emphasize that in sharing with the person they should focus on what they believe to be truth. If some of your D-Team members are nonbelievers, encourage them to study the passages again this week.

. . . With Accountability
Have your D-Team members form pairs to become accountability partners for the week and to work on the memory verse. Have each student begin learning the **Unit Memory Verse** by writing it out in the space provided in the Student Notes.

Prayer
Bring the students back together and close in prayer.

MAKE AN IMPACT

. . . In Your Life
The challenge this week is to sit down with another believer and walk the person through the steps you recorded in your Bible. Try to focus on what you believe to be truth. If you are still seeking and not sure if you believe everything that you learned today, then study the passages again this week.

. . . With Accountability
With your accountability partner, talk about your responses to the "Reflection" questions. Exchange phone numbers. Call each other this week to hold each other accountable to making an impact in your life.

name	phone

Begin learning your memory verse by writing it out in the space below.

MEMORY VERSE
Romans 1:16

1. Fishing Tackle

Preview
As you work together through "Unit 2: Fishing for Friends," you will learn how to evangelize by answering three crucial questions: "What do you believe?" "What should you say?" and "What is the power source?"

Unit Memory Verse
"I am not ashamed of the Gospel, because it is the power of God for the salvation of everyone who believes: first for the Jew, then for the Gentile" (Rom. 1:16).

Focus
Today you will answer the question, "What do you believe?" by understanding and affirming five statements of faith.

THE EXPERIENCE

Read Luke 5:1–11. What did the disciples need in order to catch men?

What do we need to "catch" our friends?

Faith Statement #1: I believe I am a sinner.
Read Romans 3:10. Then read Romans 3:23. What do these verses indicate about our spiritual condition?

If you believe the truth you just looked at, write "I believe I am a sinner" in the space below as an affirmation of that belief.

Faith Statement #2: I believe the penalty for my sin is death.
Read Romans 6:23a. What does this verse tell us about sin?

If you honestly agree with Romans 6:23a, then write, "I believe the penalty for my sin is death" in the space below as an affirmation of that belief.

Faith Statement #3: I believe God sent his son, Jesus, to die for my sins.
Read Romans 5:6–8. What did God send Jesus to do for us?

If you agree with this belief, write, "I believe God sent his Son, Jesus, to die for my sins" in the space below as an affirmation of that belief.

Faith Statement #4: I believe Jesus conquered death, which was the penalty for my sins, by rising from the dead.
Read 1 Corinthians 15:3–5. In verse 4, what did Jesus do that was miraculous?

Do you really believe this? If you agree with this truth, write, "I believe Jesus conquered death, which was the penalty for my sins, by rising from the dead" in the space below as an affirmation of that belief.

Faith Statement #5: I believe if I confess and believe with my heart the first four statements, then I will be saved.
Read Romans 10:9–10 and Ephesians 2:8–9. According to these verses, what do we need to do in order to be saved?

If you can say that you believe these truths with your whole heart, then celebrate with your other D-Team members.

REFLECTION

Today you agreed with five statements of faith that are the basis for your relationship with Jesus. The following steps will help you when you are sharing your faith with your friends. Open your Bible and take the following steps:

Step 1: Turn to Romans 3:10. Highlight this verse and then write in the margin next to it "Romans 3:23."
Step 2: Turn to Romans 3:23. Highlight this verse and then write in the margin next to it "Romans 6:23."
Step 3: Turn to Romans 6:23. Highlight this verse and then write in the margin next to it "Romans 5:6–8."
Step 4: Turn to Romans 5:6–8. Highlight this verse and then write in the margin next to it "1 Corinthians 15:3–5."
Step 5: Turn to 1 Corinthians 15:3–5. Highlight this verse and then write in the margin next to it "Romans 10:9–10."
Step 6: Turn to Romans 10:9–10. Highlight this verse and then write in the margin next to it "Ephesians 2:8–9."
Step 7: Turn to Ephesians 2:8–9. Highlight this verse.

What was most meaningful to you about our experience today?

What does God want you to do in response?

Summary Statements

We learned today that . . .

- Five faith statements build the foundation for my faith.
- When sharing my faith with my friends, I can begin with Romans 3:10.

Fishing Stories

2

Before the D-Team Experience

LEADER DEVOTION

Take a few moments to reflect on how far God has taken you in your spiritual journey. Can you remember what you were like B.C. (Before Christ)? For some of us, it wasn't that long ago, and for others it was many years ago. A lot of things have changed in your life and you probably live very differently. Most likely you have many spiritual fishing stories you could share with your D-Team members, but that is not what we are going to do. Think back to the day you decided to become a Christian. Who was there? What were the circumstances? What did you say? Why did you make the commitment? This is the fishing story you will be sharing during this D-Team experience. Take as much time as you need to bring back to life that memory.

LOOKING AHEAD

Student Focus
D-Team members will answer the question, "What should I say?" by preparing to share their faith with their friends as they work through a three step plan:

Step #1: Write out your story.
Step #2: Integrate Scripture into your story.
Step #3: Share your story with others.

Unit Memory Verse
"I am not ashamed of the Gospel, because it is the power of God for the salvation of everyone who believes: first for the Jew, then for the Gentile" (Rom. 1:16).

Practical Impact
When you get to the Reflection section of this D-Team experience, you will be handing out a lure to each of your students as a reminder that they have a spiritual fishing story they can be proud to tell to anyone who asks them.

BE PREPARED

Materials Needed
- Bibles and pens
- Duplicated Student Notes
- 3x5 notecards
- Copies of Student Notes from the previous D-Team experience ("Unit 2, #1. Fishing Tackle")
- A fishing hat
- A lure for each student (look in the sporting goods departments of discount stores like Wal-Mart, or ask around church for fishermen to donate lures they don't use)

Environment

To set up the environment for this D-Team experience, you can choose one of the following. Option 1 works in any setting; Option 2 moves the experience outside your normal setting.

Option 1: Ask a seasoned fishing expert to visit your D-Team and share a story about catching the "big one" or the "one that got away." Give the person a time limit of five minutes.

Option 2: Meet in a place that is similar to where fishing stories are usually shared—around a camp fire, around a table of food (maybe a seafood restaurant), or by a small lake or stream.

Prep Notes

Leading the D-Team Experience

(60 min. total)

GET STARTED

(5 min.)

Review

Have a student read aloud the information under "Review" in the Student Notes: ***Last week you answered the crucial question: "What do you believe?" This week you will answer the question, "What should you say?" Last week you also were challenged to walk another believer through the steps you recorded in your Bible. Share the results of this experience with the rest of the group.***

Student Prayer

Have one of your students pray that the students in the D-Team will be able to put into words how they became Christians.

Focus

Share with your group that during this D-Team experience they will answer the question, "What should I say?" by preparing to share their faith as they work through a three-step plan:

Step #1: Write out your story.
Step #2: Integrate Scripture into your story.
Step #3: Share your story with others.

THE EXPERIENCE

(40 min.)

Put on the fishing hat. Tell your students that most fishing experts have a story to tell about how they caught the "big one" or "the one that got away." If we listen to the story several times, the fish usually gets bigger and harder to catch each time the fishing story is told. The other characteristic of fishing pros is that they usually have a fishing hat with a bunch of lures hanging on it. The lures represent different stories of fishing they don't want to forget.

If you have invited a guest to share a fishing story, ask him or her to tell it now.

Continue by saying that today we will be writing our own fishing stories to share with our friends whenever the opportunities arise. But we won't carry on the tradition of exaggeration with each rendition!

Step #1: Write out your story.

Jesus made it very clear that we should always be ready to give an answer to those who want to know what makes us tick. Have a student ***read aloud 1 Peter 3:15.*** Ask: ***What is it that makes us different?***

If your students are Christians, then they all have a story to tell, no matter what the circumstances surrounding their salvation experiences. If you have D-Team members who are not Christians, encourage them to ask questions and listen to what the other students in the D-Team are talking about.

Ask: ***Describe one thing that caused you to seek God before you became a Christian.*** (You may need to help them by sharing a memory of your own.)

Prep Notes

Who influenced your decision? (Share the person who was influential in your own life.) ***When and where did you start your personal relationship with Jesus? Why did you accept Jesus into your life? What need was met? How has your relationship with Jesus changed the way that you live today?***

Step #2: Integrate Scripture into your story.
Distribute copies of the Student Notes from the previous D-Team experience. Take time to work together to insert the different passages from the "Reflection" section into your D-Team members' stories. Have your students write the verse references in the appropriate places in their new Student Notes.

Step #3: Share your story with others.
This step could be done several different ways depending on the number of students in your D-Team. If you have a large group of students, have them pair off and take turns telling their stories. If you only have four or five students, then keep everyone together to allow the whole group to hear and support each other as they share their stories. Affirm them when they are finished.

Ask volunteers to share their stories with the rest of the D-Team members. They can use their Student Notes to help them stay on track. If time is limited, then ask them to just give the Bible references for the verses rather than read each passage.

(5 min.)

REFLECTION

Give a fishing lure to each of your students. Encourage them to put their lures where others will see and ask about the story behind them. Say, "Now you have a fishing story of your own to be proud of, and there are many people that will be changed as a result of your telling your story every opportunity that God gives you. The lure will remind you to tell it often and without shame—your story is a great story!"

Give your students a few moments to record honest responses to the following questions found in their Student Notes: ***What was most meaningful to you about our experience today? What does God want you to do in response?***

Ask a student to read aloud the Summary Statements in the Student Notes.

Summary Statements

We learned today that . . .

- God wants us to be prepared to give an account for the hope in our hearts.
- As believers, we all have a story to tell.
- We should be excited and proud of the story we can share.

(10 min.)

MAKE AN IMPACT

. . . In Your Life
Challenge your students to look for an opportunity during the next week to share their fishing stories with someone. It could be a friend, or maybe their mom or dad, or even a complete stranger. Encourage them to be prepared to be used by God at anytime!

Prep Notes

. . . With Accountability

Have the D-Team members form pairs to become accountability partners for the week and to work on the memory verse. Have each student write out the **Unit Memory Verse** and recite it to his or her partner.

Prayer

Bring the students back together and close in prayer.

. . . With Accountability
With your accountability partner, talk about your responses to the "Reflection" questions. Exchange phone numbers. Call each other this week to hold each other accountable to making an impact in your life.

name	phone

Review your memory verse by writing it out in the space below. Then recite it to your partner.

MEMORY VERSE
Romans 1:16

2. Fishing Stories

Review
Last week you answered the crucial question: "What do you believe?" This week you will answer the question, "What should you say?" Last week you also were challenged to walk another believer through the steps you recorded in your Bible. Share the results of this experience with the rest of the group.

Focus
During this D-Team experience you will answer the question, "What should I say?" by preparing to share your faith as you work through a three-step plan.

THE EXPERIENCE

Today you will be writing out your own fishing story about which you will be able to tell your friends whenever the opportunity arises.

Step #1: Write out your story.
Read 1 Peter 3:15. What is it that makes us different?

Describe one thing that caused you to seek God before you became a Christian.

Who influenced your decision?

When and where did you start your personal relationship with Jesus?

Why did you accept Jesus into your life? What need was met?

How has your relationship with Jesus changed the way that you live today?

Step #2: Integrate Scripture into your story.
As you look back at your Student Notes from last week, take time to insert the different passages from the "Reflection" section into your story. Write the verse references in the appropriate places in your notes above.

Step #3: Share your story with others.
Take some time to share your story with another student. You can use your Student Notes to help you stay on track. If time is limited, then just give the Bible references for the verses rather than read each passage. This is a great opportunity to practice on a group that shares the same story as you. If you can get through this step, you will feel much more relaxed when you get the opportunity to share your story with a friend!

REFLECTION

You will receive a fishing lure during this week. Put your lure where others will see and ask about the story behind it. Can you think of someone who needs to hear your story? Put some thought into how you will begin to tell that person your fishing story.

What was most meaningful to you about our experience today?

What does God want you to do in response?

Summary Statements

We learned today that . . .

- God wants us to be prepared to give an account for the hope in our hearts.
- As believers, we all have a story to tell.
- We should be excited and proud of the story we can share.

MAKE AN IMPACT

. . . In Your Life
Look for an opportunity during the next week to share your fishing story with someone. It could be a friend, or maybe your mom or dad, or even a complete stranger. Be prepared to be used by God at anytime!

3

Fishing Fuel

Before the D-Team Experience

LEADER DEVOTION

People in the world are continually looking for someone in whom they can put their trust. Unfortunately, they will never find that person until they meet Jesus Christ. If you have experienced God's power in your life just once, then you know that nothing else can match the way God changes a heart. We can talk to people about changing their lives, but when we invite God's power into the relationship, He changes the picture completely.

Only God can change a heart. Do you really believe that? Until you do, you cannot be an effective witness for Jesus Christ. You will waste a lot of time trying to do the very thing only God can do. In order to help your students understand and believe what you teach them, you must believe it yourself. Take as much time as you need, then begin preparing for your D-Team experience.

LOOKING AHEAD

Student Focus
Every D-Team member will answer the question, "What is the power source?" by answering two life-changing questions:

Question #1: What is the true power source?
Question #2: How do we tap into it?

Unit Memory Verse
"I am not ashamed of the Gospel, because it is the power of God for the salvation of everyone who believes: first for the Jew, then for the Gentile" (Romans 1:16).

Practical Impact
By the end of this D-Team experience, your students will discover that only God can change their hearts. Your students will see or try their hand at fishing and know that there is nothing that they can do to cause the fish to take the bait. It is left up to chance. You will be comparing that with how your students can rely on God to entice their friends to take the bait of the Gospel.

BE PREPARED

Materials Needed
- Bibles and pens
- Duplicated Student Notes
- Fishing paraphenalia—poles, nets, lures (Option 1)
- Fishing poles, bait, and a net (Option 2)

Special Preparation

- Be prepared to share with your students a time when you experienced God's power while sharing your faith.
- For Option 2, make sure you and your students (if they decide to fish) have fishing licenses and permission to fish in the area.

Environment

To set up the environment for this D-Team experience, you can choose one of the following. Option 1 works in any setting; Option 2 moves the experience outside your normal setting.

Option 1: Continue the fishing motif by displaying fishing paraphenalia in your meeting place.

Option 2: Actually go fishing in a small lake, stream, or pond.

Prep Notes

Leading the D-Team Experience

(60 min. total)

GET STARTED

(5 min.)

Review

Have a student read aloud the information under "Review" in the Student Notes: ***Last week you answered the crucial question, "What should you say?" and worked through a three-step plan for sharing your faith. Did you share your story with anyone since last week?***

Student Prayer

Have a freshman in your group pray for a better understanding of God's power.

Focus

Share with your group that during this D-Team experience they will answer the question, "What is the power source?" Your students will be able to share their faith with their friends by answering two life-changing questions:

Question #1: What is the true power source?
Question #2: How do we tap into it?

THE EXPERIENCE

(40 min.)

If you have ever gone fishing then you know that there is no guarantee that you will catch anything. You never know if the fish will be there, if they will be hungry, or if they will want your bait. You can have all the right equipment and go to a famous fishing hole well-stocked with fish, but your chances of coming home with a huge catch are still limited.

If you are meeting by water, have a student try his or her hand at fishing if possible. Then ask: ***What makes a fish take the bait?*** Point out that during the last two D-Team experiences, your students have learned that to become fishers of friends they must know what they believe and what they should say. But even with these two tools, they still have no guarantees of catching anything. Explain that this D-Team experience will help them see that, unlike fishing for fish, fishing for friends does not have to be left up to chance. There is another resource that can be tapped that will remove the mystery and replace it with faith.

Question #1: What is the true power source?

Have one of your D-Team members ***read aloud 1 Corinthians 3:5–9.*** Then discuss the following questions: ***What images did Paul use to describe his work? What do you think the images mean? What was the true source of growth? Who have been the planters and waterers in your spiritual journey? How would you describe Paul's role? How would you describe God's role? What role do you have in sharing your faith with your friends? What role will God play?***

Now ask: ***What is the true power source?*** (God is the only Person with the power to change hearts.)

Have your D-Team members ***read Acts 3:1–13, 16 and Acts 4:5–10.*** Then discuss the following: ***What happened to the crippled beggar? Describe the roles played by Peter and John. According to these two apostles, who was responsible for the beggar's healing?*** (Jesus, the Power Source)

Prep Notes

Share with your D-Team members a time when you experienced God's power while sharing your faith.

Question #2: How do we tap into it?
It sounds too simple, but the answer to this life-changing question—How do we tap into it?—is prayer. "Pray about what?" your students may ask. Here are some answers for their question:

- ***Ask for God's power to speak* to *you and* through *you.***
- ***Ask for God's power to use what is said to touch your friend's heart.***
- ***Ask for God's power to soften and change your friend's heart.***

Ask a D-Team member to ***read aloud Romans 10:1.*** Ask: ***What key does Paul give us regarding tapping into God's power?***

(5 min.)

REFLECTION

Ask: ***Paul said his "heart's desire and prayer to God" was for the Israelites to be saved. Who is the recipient of your heart's desire and prayer to God for salvation?*** Have your students share specific names and a little background on the persons. Spend the remaining time praying for those who are named. Encourage your students to pray aloud and lift up their friends in prayer.

Give your students a few moments to record honest responses to the following questions found in their Student Notes: ***What was most meaningful to you about our experience today? What does God want you to do in response?***

Ask a student to read aloud the Summary Statements in the Student Notes.

Summary Statements

We learned today that . . .

- We do not have the power to change our friends' hearts.
- God is the source of power that will change our friends' lives.
- We can tap into God's power through prayer.

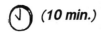

(10 min.)

MAKE AN IMPACT

. . . In Your Life
Challenge your students to record in their Student Notes the names of friends or family whom they want to see saved. Ask them to commit to spending five minutes a day praying for them. Suggest that they pick a specific time when all your D-Team members can pray no matter where they are or what they are doing. Or they could get together at school and pray for their friends on the list.

. . . With Accountability
Have the D-Team members form pairs to become accountability partners for the week and to work on the memory verse. Have each student write out the **Unit Memory Verse**, recite it to his or her partner, and share a way the verse is meaningful in his or her life.

Prayer
Bring the students back together and close in prayer.

space below.

Commit to spending five minutes a day praying for the people whose names you recorded. Pick a specific time when all your friends can pray no matter where they are or what they are doing. Or you could get together at school and pray for the people on your list.

. . . With Accountability
With your accountability partner, talk about your responses to the "Reflection" questions. Exchange phone numbers. Call each other this week to hold each other accountable to making an impact in your life.

name	phone

Review your memory verse by writing it out in the space below. After reciting it to your partner, share a way the verse is meaningful in your life.

MEMORY VERSE
Romans 1:16

3. Fishing Fuel

Review
Last week you answered the crucial question, "What should you say?" and worked through a three-step plan for sharing your faith. Did you share your story with anyone since last week?

Focus
Today you will answer the question, "What is the power source?" You will be able to share your faith with your friends by answering two life-changing questions.

THE EXPERIENCE

What makes a fish take the bait?

Question #1: What is the true power source?
Read 1 Corinthians 3:5–9. Then answer the following questions:

What images did Paul use to describe his work? What do you think the images mean?

What was the true source of growth?

Who have been the planters and waterers in *your* spiritual journey?

How would you describe Paul's role? How would you describe God's role?

What role do you have in sharing your faith with your friends? What role will God play?

What is the true power source?

Read Acts 3:1–13, 16 and Acts 4:5–10. Then answer the following questions:

What happened to the crippled beggar?

Describe the roles played by Peter and John.

According to these two apostles, who was responsible for the beggar's healing?

Question #2: How do we tap into it?
It sounds too simple, but the answer to this life-changing question is prayer. "Pray about what?" you may ask. Here are some answers for your question:

- Ask for God's power to speak *to* you and *through* you.
- Ask for God's power to use what is said to touch your friend's heart.
- Ask for God's power to soften and change your friend's heart.

Read Romans 10:1. What key does Paul give us regarding tapping into God's power?

REFLECTION

Paul said his "heart's desire and prayer to God" was for the Israelites to be saved. Who are the recipients of your heart's desire and prayer to God for salvation?

Share specific names and a little background on the persons with the group. Spend the remaining time praying for those who are named. Pray aloud and lift up your friends in prayer.

What was most meaningful to you about our experience today?

What does God want you to do in response?

Summary Statements

We learned today that . . .

- We do not have the power to change our friends' hearts.
- God is the source of power that will change our friends' lives.
- We can tap into God's power through prayer.

MAKE AN IMPACT

. . . In Your Life
Record the names of friends or family whom you want to see saved in the

1,2,3 COMBINATIONS

STUDENT IMPACT

Unit 3 Introduction

LEADER FOCUS

Jesus told His followers: "Greater love has no one than this, that he lay down his life for his friends" (John 15:13). What does this passage mean to you? Would you be willing to give your life for your friends? Why is it so hard for some of us to swallow our insecurities and witness to our friends? Spend some time praying for your friends, and then pray for the students in your D-Team. This unit gives specific instructions on how to evangelize, beginning with making non-Christian friends. Pray that the Holy Spirit will take control of your students and use each one to witness to the world.

BIG PICTURE

Unit Overview

In Unit 3 you will be focusing on accomplishing one goal—teaching your students the specific steps to take in order to reach the unreached. The first D-Team experience will help your students discover how to develop integrity friendships. The second D-Team experience will help your students discover specific instructions for sharing a verbal witness. The third D-Team experience will help your students discover how to use a supplemental witness with their friends.

1. Integrity Friendships

During this D-Team experience, your students will discover how to develop integrity friendships by answering three simple questions:

Question #1: What is an integrity friendship?
Question #2: Why do we need integrity friendships?
Question #3: How do we develop integrity friendships?

2. A Verbal Witness

During this D-Team experience, your students will discover how to share a verbal witness by taking three steps:

Step #1: Describe the life you used to know.
Step #2: Describe your decision.
Step #3: Describe your new life.

3. A Supplemental Witness

During this D-Team experience, your students will discover how to share a supplemental witness after they have shared Christ verbally with a friend. They will do this by taking three steps:

Step #1: Direct your friends.
Step #2: Challenge your friends.
Step #3: Support your friends.

Unit Memory Verse
"But in your hearts set apart Christ as Lord. Always be prepared to give an answer to everyone who asks you to give the reason for the hope that you have" (1 Peter 3:15–16).

Integrity Friendships

1

Before the D-Team Experience

LEADER DEVOTION

"As iron sharpens iron, so one man sharpens another" (Prov. 27:17).

Are you doing all you can to build up God's kingdom? Before you ask your students to focus on integrity friendships, think of the friendships in your own life. Are you involved in relationships right now which you know are not pleasing to God? Do you have selfish motives in your relationships?

Be quiet for a moment and reflect on your relationships. Pray that God will take you out of unhealthy relationships. Ask God to help you build new friendships in which you will be an honest, unselfish, credible friend who is willing to be used as a candle, spreading His light to every dark corner of the world.

LOOKING AHEAD

Student Focus

Every D-Team member will discover how to develop integrity friendships by answering three simple questions:

Question #1: What is an integrity friendship?
Question #2: Why do we need integrity friendships?
Question #3: How do we develop integrity friendships?

Unit Memory Verse

"But in your hearts set apart Christ as Lord. Always be prepared to give an answer to everyone who asks you to give the reason for the hope that you have" (1 Peter 3:15–16).

Practical Impact

During this D-Team experience, you will give a pet rock to each of your students. This rock will symbolize the type of friend they do *not* want to be. They will use this rock to remind them of what it means to be a real friend as opposed to a mere rock.

BE PREPARED

Materials Needed

- Bibles and pens
- Duplicated Student Notes
- A small rock for each D-Team member
- Colored markers

Environment

To set up the environment for this D-Team experience, you can choose one of the following. Option 1 works in any setting; Option 2 moves the experience outside your normal setting.

Option 1: Begin your D-Team experience with a story from your own life about a friendship and what made it so special. Bring in pictures or keepsakes from that relationship. Or, contact a student and ask him or her to be prepared to tell about a special friendship in his or her life. Another idea would be to bring in a clip from the movie *Beaches* or *The Outsiders* or the TV show *Friends.* Have your students discuss what makes these relationships "stick."

Option 2: Take your students to their high school campus, workplace, or athletic field. Ask them to reminisce about the relationships they have developed in this place. Ask if they have any regrets regarding their ability to be a true friend.

Prep Notes

Leading the D-Team Experience

(60 min. total)

GET STARTED

(5 min.)

Unit Preview

Have a student read aloud the following information from the "Preview" in the Student Notes: ***As you work together through "Unit 3: 1, 2, 3 Combinations," you will learn how to help an unchurched person become a believer in Christ. You will do this by discovering how to develop integrity friendships, how to share a verbal witness, and how to share a supplemental witness.***

Unit Memory Verse

Read aloud 1 Peter 3:15–16: "But in your hearts set apart Christ as Lord. Always be prepared to give an answer to everyone who asks you to give the reason for the hope that you have." Explain that in this letter Peter encouraged Jewish and Gentile Christians to make an inner commitment to Christ.

Student Prayer

Ask a student to pray that each person will come to a fuller understanding of what it means to develop integrity friendships.

Focus

Share with your D-Team members that this week they will discover how to develop integrity friendships by answering three simple questions:

Question #1: What is an integrity friendship?
Question #2: Why do we need integrity friendships?
Question #3: How do we develop integrity friendships?

THE EXPERIENCE

(40 min.)

What is an integrity friendship?

After you and your students have shared stories of powerful friendships, ask your students to write down a response to the following question: ***What one characteristic would you consider essential in a friend?*** Give an example such as honesty or unselfishness. After they have finished, have them share their answer. Don't forget to ask why they think that particular characteristic is important.

Ask your students to ***define the word* integrity**. After they have shared their definitions, read the following definition and have them record it in their Student Notes: *Integrity is completeness, wholeness, unimpaired condition, honesty, or sincerity.*

Emphasize that the Book of Proverbs has a lot to say about friendship. Assign each student one of the following verses. Instruct them to read their assigned verses silently and jot down what their verses have to say about integrity friendships:

Proverbs 3:27–28 (Don't withhold good from your friends.)
Proverbs 16:28 (Don't stir up trouble or gossip.)
Proverbs 18:1 (Don't pursue selfish ends.)

Prep Notes

Proverbs 18:24 (Don't spread yourself too thin.)
Proverbs 25:20 (Be there when friends are down.)
Proverbs 26:18–19 (Don't deceive your friends.)
Proverbs 28:23 (Don't practice flattery.)
Proverbs 27:9–10 (Don't forsake your friends.)

Why do we need integrity friendships?
Have a student ***read aloud Matthew 22:37–39***. Ask them to discuss with a partner: ***Why do you think loving our neighbors is such an important commandment?*** Have each pair share their thoughts with the rest of the students. If none of the students mentions it, point out that we can't be effective witnesses if we don't treat others with respect.

Read Ecclesiastes 4:7–12 and ask: ***What can we learn about friendship from these verses?***

Help students visualize what you are saying by painting this word picture: Imagine you are a farmer getting ready to plant your crop. If you were to walk on the field and just pour seed all over the land, your crop would more than likely fail. Before you can plant the seeds, you need to cultivate the land. You need to prepare it for the seeds you will plant. In the same way, we need to develop integrity friendships before we plant the seed of the Gospel. People will be more inclined to listen to a radical message from a trusted friend than from a stranger.

How do we develop integrity friendships?
Now that your students have discussed what integrity friendships are and why we need them, it is time to work on some practical applications of how to develop integrity friendships.

Point students to the word ***"FRIEND"*** written vertically in their student notes. As a group, decide on a characteristic of integrity friendship for each letter. For example:

F faithful
R respectful
I interested in others
E encouraging
N non-critical
D devoted

Encourage students to use the acronym they develop as a model for relating to one another within the D-Team as well as in their other friendships.

(5 min.)

REFLECTION

Give each student a rock. Remind them that there was a time when pet rocks were popular. What would it be like if a rock were your best friend? What qualities would be missing from that friendship? Point out that sometimes we tend to be more like rocks than like integrity friends when we feel the pressures of time, school work, and so on.

Hand out markers and ask students to choose two characteristics of a true friend (from the FRIEND acronym, or other ideas they might have) they want to work on. Have them write the characteristics on their rocks. Suggest that they place their rocks in their lockers, or somewhere that will remind them of the kind of friends they want to be.

Give your students a few moments to record honest responses to the following questions found on their Student Notes: ***What was most meaningful to you about our experience today? What does God want you to do in response?***

Prep Notes

Ask a student to read aloud the Summary Statements in the Student Notes.

Summary Statements
We learned today that . . . • We are called to share the Gospel with others. • Before we can witness to others, we must develop integrity friendships. • A good friend is honest, unselfish, encouraging, and willing to sacrifice. • In order to develop integrity relationships, we must develop these characteristics.

MAKE AN IMPACT

(10 min.)

. . . In Your Life

Challenge your students to make a personal plan to develop an integrity friendship. Urge them to pray that God will make clear to them the areas that need to be "fixed" in order for them to become true friends. Encourage them to read about two amazing friendships in the Bible:

- David and Jonathan—1 Samuel 20
- Ruth and Naomi—the Book of Ruth

. . . With Accountability

Have your D-Team members form pairs to become accountability partners for the week, and to work on the memory verse. Have each student begin learning the **Unit Memory Verse** by writing it out in the space provided in the Student Notes.

Prayer

Bring the students back together and close in prayer.

Find time this week to read about two amazing friendships in the Bible:

- David and Jonathan—1 Samuel 20
- Ruth and Naomi—the Book of Ruth

. . . With Accountability
With your accountability partner, talk about your responses to the "Reflection" questions. Exchange phone numbers. Call each other this week to hold each other accountable to making an impact in your life.

name	phone

Begin learning your memory verse by writing it out in the space below.

MEMORY VERSE
1 Peter 3:15–16

1. Integrity Friendships

Preview
As you work together through "Unit 3: 1, 2, 3 Combinations," you will learn how to help an unchurched person become a believer in Christ. You will do this by discovering how to develop integrity friendships, how to share a verbal witness, and how to share a supplemental witness.

Unit Memory Verse
"But in your hearts set apart Christ as Lord. Always be prepared to give an answer to everyone who asks you to give the reason for the hope that you have" (1 Peter 3:15–16).

Focus
This week, you will discover how to develop integrity friendships by answering three simple questions.

THE EXPERIENCE

What is an integrity friendship?
Share a story of a powerful friendship.

What one characteristic would you consider essential in a friend?

Define the word *integrity*.

The Book of Proverbs has a lot to say about friendship. Silently read your assigned verses and prepare to share what your verses have to say about integrity friendships:

Proverbs 3:27–28

Proverbs 16:28

Proverbs 18:1

Proverbs 18:24

Proverbs 25:20

Proverbs 26:18–19

Proverbs 28:23

Proverbs 27:9–10

Why do we need integrity friendships?
Read Matthew 22:37–39. Why do you think loving our neighbors is such an important commandment?

Read Ecclesiastes 4:7–12. What can we learn about friendship from these verses?

How do we develop integrity friendships?
F
R
I
E
N
D

REFLECTION

You have discussed many characteristics of an integrity friendship. Choose two character traits to develop in your life that will make you a better friend. Use a marker to write the two character traits on your rock. Take this rock home and place it where you can see it as a reminder to develop into the best friend you can be, so that God can use you to bring others into His kingdom.

What was most meaningful to you about our experience today?

What does God want you to do in response?

Summary Statements

We learned today that . . .
- We are called to share the Gospel with others.
- Before we can witness to others, we must develop integrity friendships.
- A good friend is honest, unselfish, encouraging, and willing to sacrifice.
- In order to develop integrity relationships, we must develop these characteristics.

MAKE AN IMPACT

. . . In Your Life
This week, take time to make a personal plan to develop an integrity friendship. Pray that God will make clear to you the areas of your life that need to be "fixed" in order for you to become a true friend.

2

A Verbal Witness

Before the D-Team Experience

LEADER DEVOTION

Read and reflect on Psalm 130. Focus on this phrase: "If you, O Lord, kept a record of sins, O Lord, who could stand?" (Ps. 130:3). Think about this for a moment. Although it often seems we are not worthy of the unfailing and redeeming love of Christ, He has offered it to us if we are willing to accept it. How can we share this Good News with others?

As you prepare to help your students learn how to share a verbal witness, think about the words that made the Good News "click" for you. Then pray for each of your D-Team members. Ask the Holy Spirit to fill each student with the courage and the words to be a verbal witness. Ask that opportunities will arise for students to be verbal witnesses. Also pray for the friends of your students. Ask that they will have open ears and hearts. Lastly, pray that you will not become too comfortable in your faith. Ask for the feeling of urgency to always be upon you so that you will continually seek out opportunities to share the hope that you have.

LOOKING AHEAD

Student Focus
Every D-Team member will discover how to share a verbal witness by taking three steps:

Step #1: Describe the life you used to know.
Step #2: Describe your decision.
Step #3: Describe your new life.

Unit Memory Verse
"But in your hearts set apart Christ as Lord. Always be prepared to give an answer to everyone who asks you to give the reason for the hope that you have" (1 Peter 3:15–16).

Practical Impact
At the end of this D-Team experience, your students will have the experience of holding a candle and setting the room ablaze with light. This is symbolic of the light we are called to shine across the land. The students will experience just how to ignite the fire through words.

BE PREPARED

Materials Needed
- Bibles and pens
- Duplicated Student Notes
- A candle for each D-Team member
- Matches

Special Preparation

- Draw a picture or a symbol of what your life has been like since making the decision to follow Christ. Be prepared to share your own picture or symbol with your students.
- For Option 1: Call students and ask them to bring their yearbooks, team pictures, or group shots of friends.

Environment

To set up the environment for this D-Team experience, you can choose one of the following. Option 1 works in any setting; Option 2 moves the experience outside your normal setting.

Option 1: Have students bring in their yearbooks, team pictures, or group shots of friends. Have the students decide with which of these people they have developed integrity friendships. Inquire whether your students are ready to take the "next step" with those people.

Option 2: Take your students to a court house. Have the students discuss what it means to be a witness in our judicial system. You might discuss the O.J. Simpson trial or another famous case. Help your students realize that a witness is one who saw or can give a firsthand account. Inquire whether your students are ready to be witnesses to their friends.

Prep Notes

Leading the D-Team Experience

(60 min. total)

GET STARTED

(5 min.)

Review

Have a student read aloud the information under "Review" in the Student Notes: ***Last week you took the first step in evangelism. You learned that an integrity friendship is based on honesty, unselfishness, encouragement, and a willingness to sacrifice. It is important that we build these relationships so our friends will trust us when we share the Good News about Jesus Christ with them. This week you will be reaching out to those friends by sharing a verbal witness.***

Student Prayer

Ask a student to pray that each D-Team member will come to a fuller understanding of *how* to become a verbal witness.

Focus

Share with your group that during this D-Team experience they will discover how to share a verbal witness by taking three steps:

Step #1: Describe the life you used to know.
Step #2: Describe your decision.
Step #3: Describe your new life.

THE EXPERIENCE

(40 min.)

Begin your D-Team experience by turning off the lights and having your students put their heads down and close their eyes. Tell your students to use their imaginations while you take them on a "ride." Paint the following word picture for them: You are traveling in an airplane with all of your friends. Suddenly the pilot says to prepare for a crash landing. The plane is heading straight for the ground at an amazing speed. (Long pause) You are now walking in the most beautiful place you can imagine. You realize you are holding hands with Jesus. Suddenly, He stops and looks into your eyes and with a soft voice says to you, "Welcome home, My child. It's wonderful to see you, but tell me one thing—Did you tell your friends about Me?"

Read the following poem to your students:

My friend I stand in judgment now
and feel that you're to blame, somehow;
on earth you walked with me everyday
but never did you point the way.
—Anonymous

Then tell your students that we are called to be witnesses to our friends. At times this can seem like a "mission impossible," but there are three steps to follow which make sharing the Good News about Christ a little easier.

Step #1: Describe the life you used to know.

Explain to your students that before they can tell their friends *how* to become a

Prep Notes

Christian, they must explain *why*. Imagine a doctor announcing that he has just found a cure to the "Zombie Virus." Before you run out and get a shot, you would want to know exactly *what* this virus was, and *why* you needed a shot. Sharing a verbal witness with our friends is very similar in that we must start by explaining to our friends that they have a need and we know a cure.

Have a student read aloud Romans 3:9–18. The Bible makes it very clear that we all have a disease—we are all sinners. Remind your students, however, that it might sound too condemning and judgmental to get right in a friend's face and accuse them of sinning. Tell your students that the best way to explain the need without coming across too harsh is to give a personal example. They can do this by explaining the sin and the need that existed in their own lives before they met Christ. This is called "Describing the life you knew." Have your students fill in the following questions found in their Student Notes.

What was your life like before you met Christ?

What sin was in your life?

What pain was in your life?

What wants or needs weren't being met?

Now ask three students to read aloud the following verses. Have all the students write a summary statement after each reference.

- ***Romans 3:23***—All have sinned and fall short of God's glory.
- ***Romans 5:12***—Death spread because all have sinned.
- ***1 John 1:8***—If we say we have no sin, we are deceiving ourselves.

Tell your students that they can use these verses to support their case in Step #1 of sharing a verbal witness.

Now it is time for role-playing. Have each student select a partner (triads will work, too). Tell them, "Now I am going to give you the opportunity to practice the first step of sharing a verbal witness. One of you will play the role of a nonbeliever, and the other will share a verbal witness. If you are playing the nonbeliever, be sure to be creative in your role. Remember that people respond in many different ways. If you are the believer, pretend that you have already developed an integrity friendship with this person. He or she is now ready for you to convince him or her that he or she has a need. Do this by describing the life you led before you came into a relationship with Jesus Christ. You might want to use some or all of the verses from Romans and 1 John to enhance your point. Remember to be very sensitive to how your partner is responding to you."

Give students a few minutes to role-play, then have them switch roles, so that each student has a chance to practice describing the life he or she used to know.

Step #2: Describe your decision.
Ask several students to ***read aloud the following verses.*** Have all the students write a summary statement after each reference.

- ***Matthew 4:17***—Repent because God's reign in the person and ministry of Jesus Christ is in effect.
- ***John 3:16***—Whoever believes in Jesus shall have eternal life.
- ***John 14:6***—Jesus is the way, the truth, and the life.
- ***Acts 2:38–39***—Repent and you shall receive the gift of the Holy Spirit.
- ***Romans 6:23***—The penalty for sin is death.

Prep Notes

Point out that these verses all describe a choice that has been given to each of us. Say, "The next step in sharing a verbal witness is to present this decision to your friend. This is done by sharing a personal example of what has happened in your own life. Be very clear in explaining exactly what this decision is all about. The questions you should cover are: ***What was the decision I had to make? Why did I make the decision I made? What other choice did I have? Who or what was the biggest influence on my decision?"***

Now have the students take about five to eight minutes to write a description of the decision they made. If time permits, have some of the students share their answers aloud. Be sure they understand that because Christ died on the cross we have a decision to make—we can either accept or reject His free gift of eternal life.

Step #3: Describe your new life.
The third step in sharing a verbal witness is the "So what?" or "What's next?" of Christianity. Tell your students that this step is often overlooked. Explain that often people get so excited when a friend is receptive to making a decision, they forget to tell the person what happens next.

In their Student Notes, have your students describe their new lives since following Christ. Suggest that they draw a picture or a symbol of what their life has been like since making the decision to follow Christ. If some of your students claim to be "artistically challenged," allow them to make a list of adjectives describing their new lives. Help your students understand that the description of their new life should be very positive. So often people are turned off by Christianity because they are under the impression that it is just a list of do's and don'ts. Have your students read the following verses that express what happens in the "new life":

- ***Matthew 6:33***—Seek first the kingdom of Christ.
- ***Romans 6:1–14***—We are dead to our old selves and now have a newness of life.
- ***2 Corinthians 4:16–18***—What is seen is temporary; what is unseen is eternal.
- ***2 Corinthians 5:17***—We are a new creation.

Be prepared to share your own picture or symbol. When everyone is finished, have volunteers share their drawings or lists.

REFLECTION

(5 min.)

Have your students get in a circle. As they are doing this, turn out the lights and make the room as dark as possible. Tell the students that this is symbolic of Step #1 in sharing a verbal witness—describing the life we knew. Then give each student a candle. Note that accepting the candle is symbolic of Step #2 in sharing a verbal witness—describing our decision. Next, light your candle and then use your candle to light a student's candle. Have your students pass the flame around the circle until everyone's candle has been lit. Point out that the light is symbolic of Step #3 in sharing a verbal witness—describing our new lives. Ask your students to look around the room and notice what a difference can be made in the world if we share verbal witnesses.

Give your students a few moments to record honest responses to the following questions found in their Student Notes: ***What was most meaningful to you about our experience today? What does God want you to do in response?***

Ask a student to read aloud the Summary Statements in the Student Notes.

Prep Notes

Summary Statements

We learned today that . . .

- After we develop integrity friendships, the next step is to share a verbal witness by:
  Describing the lives we knew.
  Describing our decision.
  Describing our new lives.
- Following these steps is one more move we can make to bring our friends to Christ.

(10 min.)

MAKE AN IMPACT

. . . In Your Life

Challenge your students to read Colossians 4:2–6 this week. Urge them to spend time praying for boldness and for opportunities as they become verbal witnesses to their friends.

. . . With Accountability

Have the D-Team members form pairs to become accountability partners for the week and to work on the memory verse. Have each student write out the **Unit Memory Verse** and recite it to his or her partner.

Prayer

Bring the students back together and close in prayer.

name	phone

Review your memory verse by writing it out in the space below. Then recite it to your partner.

MEMORY VERSE

1 Peter 3:15–16

2. A Verbal Witness

Review

Last week you took the first step in evangelism. You learned that an integrity friendship is based on honesty, unselfishness, encouragement, and a willingness to sacrifice. It is important that we build these relationships so our friends will trust us when we share the Good News about Jesus Christ with them. This week you will be reaching out to those friends by sharing a verbal witness.

Focus

Today, you will discover how to share a verbal witness by taking three steps.

THE EXPERIENCE

Step #1: Describe the life you used to know.

What was your life like before you met Christ?

What sin was in your life?

What pain was in your life?

What wants or needes weren't being met?

Read the following verses and jot a summary statement after each reference:

- Romans 3:23
- Romans 5:12
- 1 John 1:8

Step #2: Describe your decision.
Read the following verses and jot a summary statement after each reference:

- Matthew 4:17
- John 3:16
- John 14:6
- Acts 2:38–39
- Romans 6:23

Describe your decision to follow Christ. What was the decision you had to make? Why did you make the decision you made? What other choice did you have? Who or what was the biggest influence on your decision? Be prepared to share your description.

Step #3: Describe your new life.
Describe your new life since following Christ. Draw a picture or a symbol of what your life has been like since making the decision to follow Christ. If you consider yourself "artistically challenged," make a list of adjectives describing your new life. Be prepared to share your drawing or list. You can get ideas from these verses, which express what happens in the "new life":

- Matthew 6:33
- Romans 6:1–14
- 2 Corinthians 4:16–18
- 2 Corinthians 5:17

REFLECTION

What was most meaningful to you about our experience today?

What does God want you to do in response?

Summary Statements

We learned today that . . .

- After we develop integrity friendships, the next step is to share a verbal witness by:
  Describing the lives we knew.
  Describing our decision.
  Describing our new lives.
- Following these steps is one more move we can make to bring our friends to Christ.

MAKE AN IMPACT

. . . In Your Life
Read Colossians 4:2–6 this week. Spend some time praying for boldness and for opportunities as you become a verbal witness to your friends. Ask the Holy Spirit to work in the hearts of these friends.

. . . With Accountability
With your accountability partner, talk about your responses to the "Reflection" questions. Exchange phone numbers. Call each other this week to hold each other accountable to making an impact in your life.

A Supplemental Witness

3

Before the D-Team Experience

LEADER DEVOTION

"He must become greater; I must become less" (John 3:30). This was John the Baptist's testimony when one of his followers asked him about Jesus. Like John, we must realize that our lives are nothing if we are not living for Christ. Before you lead your students in learning how to share a supplemental witness, think about your role on this earth. Do you think about Christ more than you think about yourself? Are you constantly seeking opportunities to bring your friends to Christ? Do you feel the urgency to spread the Gospel to every person who crosses your path? Are you on your knees daily for the lost of this world? Spend a few moments in prayer.

LOOKING AHEAD

Student Focus
Every D-Team member will discover how to share a supplemental witness by taking three steps:

Step #1: Direct your friends.
Step #2: Challenge your friends.
Step #3: Support your friends.

Unit Memory Verse
"But in your hearts set apart Christ as Lord. Always be prepared to give an answer to everyone who asks you to give the reason for the hope that you have" (1 Peter 3:15–16).

Practical Impact
At the end of this D-Team experience, your students will have the opportunity to plan an activity to which they will all bring friends.

BE PREPARED

Materials Needed

- Bibles and pens
- Duplicated Student Notes
- A calendar
- Videotape, slides, or photographs of high school activities; VCR, TV to play videotape (Option 1)

Special Preparation

- For Option 1: Put together a videotape, slides, or photographs of several high school activities that have been sponsored by your church (for example: retreats, concerts, athletic events, church services, or D-Team outings).

Environment

To set up the environment for this D-Team experience, you can choose one of the following. Option 1 works in any setting; Option 2 moves the experience outside your normal setting.

Option 1: Bring in a videotape, slides, or photographs of several high school activities that have been sponsored by your church. The purpose is to show the students that there are many places to bring unsaved friends where they will have fun and see that Christians are normal people. After you play the video or show the pictures, discuss the following questions with your students: Why are we afraid to bring friends to Christian activities? What church activity would be the best place to bring a friend? What can our church do to make it easier to bring friends? What can we as a D-Team do to make it easier to bring friends?

Option 2: Take your D-Team members to a place where they have fun together. You might take them outside for a quick game of football or soccer. You could bring a sprinkler for them to run through. Or you might take them for doughnuts or to a park. The purpose is to show your students that even though they have this common bond of Christ, they still are normal people who like to have fun.

Prep Notes

Leading the D-Team Experience

(60 min. total)

GET STARTED

(5 min.)

Review

Have a student read aloud the information under "Review" in the Student Notes: ***For the past two weeks, we have talked about the relational steps that are taken in evangelism. First we learned of the need to build integrity friendships. Then we discussed how to share a verbal witness. This week we will take the next step—sharing a supplemental witness.***

Student Prayer

Before the prayer, go around the room and ask for names of friends your students are thinking about inviting to a special activity. Then have a student pray that each person mentioned will be receptive to the invitation.

Focus

Share with your group that during this D-Team experience they will discover how to share a supplemental witness by taking three steps:

Step #1: Direct your friends.
Step #2: Challenge your friends.
Step #3: Support your friends.

THE EXPERIENCE

(40 min.)

Begin this D-Team experience by asking your students to ***define the word* supplemental.** After a brief discussion, ask them to record the following definition in their Student Notes: *Supplemental means something added, especially to make up for a lack.*

Emphasize that this is the third step in relational evangelism. Students have already built an integrity friendship and shared a verbal witness. Now it is time to supplement all the "talk" with something visual. It is time to get their friends to come and see for themselves what it means to live with Christ.

Step #1: Direct your friends.

Suggest that before we invite our friends to an activity, we must ask ourselves two questions: What interests does our friend have? What are our options in terms of places to bring this friend? Have your students think about the friend they want to bring, and answer the following questions in their Student Notes: ***What likes/dislikes does your friend have? What gets him or her excited? What turns him or her off?***

Now that the students have thought about their friends' interests, they should focus on the options they have. In other words, ***where could they bring a friend so that he or she would feel comfortable?*** Compile a list of "Christian" places where students can bring a friend. Remind the students that they want to think of places where their friends will feel welcome, have a good time, and see how Christians interact. Some examples might be: Sunday worship service, high school program, concert, retreat, D-Team meeting, service project, etc.

Prep Notes

After making the list, have a student ***read aloud 2 Corinthians 4:1–5.*** Spend a few moments discussing this passage. Ask: ***How might a ministry use deception or distort the word of God? Why is it important to set forth the truth plainly? How might we set forth the truth plainly and yet still have a service that is fun? What does it mean "to commend ourselves to every man's conscience in the sight of God"?***

Help your students see that, when we direct our friends, we want to direct them to a place where the truth is not distorted and where Christians are friendly and know how to have fun. Remind your students that the two keys to the first step (direct your friends) are to know what your friend likes/dislikes and to know several options of places where you can bring that friend.

Step #2: Challenge your friends.
Now that your students have thought about how and where to direct their friends, they need to focus on how to go about challenging them. Ask your students: ***Imagine you are going to throw a big party and want lots of people to show up. How would you go about accomplishing this?*** As your students share their responses, make sure you mention these three things: (1) send a party invitation, (2) ask for a response, and (3) remind or confirm the date with your guest.

It is no different when we think of inviting our friends to church. Many of us think that if we pray and wait long enough our friends will come to us. How many times have friends ever come to you and asked if they could come to a party before you invited them? The time is now, and we must make the invitation.

Ask a student to ***read aloud Jeremiah 20:7–9.*** Introduce this passage by explaining that Jeremiah was a prophet who had just been beaten and placed in the stocks. Here he speaks out against the priest who put him there. Have your D-Team members pair off and work together to ***summarize these verses.*** Explain that, like Jeremiah, we might be ridiculed for what we have to say, but that should not stop us. Our invitations to our friends should be like a fire in our bones that will explode if we do not let it out.

Tell your students that it is not enough that we give an invitation. We must ask our friends to give us an answer. Have your students do some role-playing about inviting a friend to a church-related activity. Remind the students to give invitations that are both specific and appealing. Remind the students to be prepared for questions their friends may have.

Step #3: Support your friends.
Remind your students: ***The first step in sharing a supplemental witness is to know how and where to direct your friends, and the second step is to challenge them or invite them. The third step in a supplemental witness is to support and encourage friends.***

Ask a student to ***read aloud Philippians 2:1–4.*** Have a student summarize how these verses can apply to sharing a supplemental witness. Emphasize that our motivation for bringing friends is not to make ourselves look better or earn some kind of spiritual "points." Rather, we should bring and encourage friends because we are looking out for what is best for them: to come to know Christ.

Ask your students to think about the following questions: ***In what ways can you support your friends unselfishly? What are some ways you might encourage your friends after having invited them?*** For example, they could call them, remind them in school, have them bring another friend so they don't feel alone, spend time talking to that person once you get them to the activity, tell their other friends to make

Prep Notes

this person feel at home when they bring him or her. Remind your students that support is probably the most important step. Tell them to think how it would feel to go to a church for the first time and feel all alone. Remind them that, as D-Team members, it is their responsibility to support any friends that a fellow D-Team member might bring.

REFLECTION

(5 min.)

Now that you have discussed the three steps to sharing a supplemental witness, have your students plan an activity to put the steps into practice. Have them choose an activity and set a date. Take the next few minutes to plan out an activity, such as a shopping spree, trip to an amusement park, trip to the zoo, athletic contest, etc. Remind your students to consider their friends' interests. Once they agree on a date, have them make all the arrangements. Remind the students to promote the activity so that their friends will want to come.

Give your students a few moments to record honest responses to the following questions found in their Student Notes: ***What was most meaningful to you about our experience today? What does God want you to do in response?***

Ask a student to read aloud the Summary Statements in the Student Notes.

Summary Statements

We learned today that . . .

- It is important that we share a supplemental witness so that, after our friends have heard our words in a verbal witness, they can see firsthand what Christians are really like.
- In order to share a supplemental witness, we must direct, challenge, and support our friends.

MAKE AN IMPACT

(10 min.)

. . . In Your Life

Challenge your students to read 1 Corinthians 15:58 this week. As they are inviting and encouraging their friends, they need to remember that everyone won't say yes. Remind them that Satan doesn't want our friends to come. Urge students to spend time in prayer that they will be able to encourage their friends in the way they need to be encouraged.

. . . With Accountability

Have the D-Team members form pairs to become accountability partners for the week and to work on the memory verse. Have each student write out the **Unit Memory Verse**, recite it to his or her partner, and share a way the verse is meaningful in his or her life.

Prayer

Bring the students back together and close in prayer.

Summary Statements

We learned today that . . .

- It is important that we share a supplemental witness so that after our friends have heard our words in a verbal witness, they can see firsthand what Christians are really like.
- In order to share a supplemental witness, we must direct, challenge, and support our friends.

MAKE AN IMPACT

. . . In Your Life

Read 1 Corinthians 15:58 this week. As you invite and encourage your friends, remember that everyone won't say yes. Satan doesn't want your friends to come. Spend time in prayer asking God to help you encourage your friends in the way they need to be encouraged.

. . . With Accountability

With your accountability partner, talk about your responses to the "Reflection" questions. Exchange phone numbers. Call each other this week to hold each other accountable to making an impact in your life.

name	phone

Review your memory verse by writing it out in the space below. After reciting it to your partner, share a way the verse is meaningful in your life.

MEMORY VERSE

1 Peter 3:15–16

3. A Supplemental Witness

Review

For the past two weeks, we have talked about the relational steps that are taken in evangelism. First we learned of the need to build integrity friendships. Then we discussed how to share a verbal witness. This week we will take the next step—sharing a supplemental witness.

Focus

You will discover how to share a supplemental witness by taking three steps.

THE EXPERIENCE

Define the word *supplemental.*

Step #1: Direct your friends.

What likes/dislikes does your friend have?

What gets him or her excited? What turns him or her off?

Where could you bring a friend so that he or she would feel comfortable?

Read 2 Corinthians 4:1–5. How might a ministry use deception or distort the word of God?

Why is it important to set forth the truth plainly?

How might we set forth the truth plainly and yet still have a service that is fun?

What does it mean "to commend ourselves to every man's conscience in the sight of God"?

Step #2: Challenge your friends.
Imagine you are going to throw a big party and want a lot of people to show up. How would you go about accomplishing this?

Read and summarize Jeremiah 20:7–9.

Step #3: Support your friends.
The first step in sharing a supplemental witness is to know how and where to direct your friends, and the second step is to challenge them or invite them. The third step in a supplemental witness is to support and encourage friends.

Read Philippians 2:1–4. Summarize how these verses can apply to sharing a supplemental witness.

What are some ways I can support my friends unselfishly?

What are some ways I can encourage friends after I have invited them?

REFLECTION

Now that you have discussed the three steps to sharing a supplemental witness, you will plan an activity so you can put the steps into practice. Take the next few minutes to plan out an activity, such as a shopping spree, trip to an amusement park, trip to the zoo, athletic contest, etc. Consider your friends' interests. Once you agree on a date, make all the arrangements. Remember to promote the activity so that your friends will want to come.

What was most meaningful to you about our experience today?

What does God want you to do in response?

STUDENT IMPACT

TARGETS

Unit 4 Introduction

LEADER FOCUS

Remember the last project you worked hard on? How much planning did it take? Did you have a specific goal in mind? Was there a finished product you wanted to see when you completed the project? Have you ever done something without a goal or target? Was it frustrating? Did you take time to determine what your target was? Why or why not? Reflect for a moment on Christ's life. Do you think His life was lived out with an ultimate target in mind? Of course! It was you! Take some time to thank Him before you prepare to lead this unit.

BIG PICTURE

Unit Overview
Tools are items used to complete a project more efficiently and effectively. The D-Team experiences in Unit 4 will be focused on a tool we call "supplemental witness" that is used to assist a verbal witness. Each experience will help your students evangelize their friends by creating, preparing, and celebrating an event they can use as a supplemental witness. You and your students will hold this event between the second and third experiences in this unit.

1. Bull's-Eye
Targets help us focus on what we are shooting at and ultimately help us hit the bull's-eye. During this D-Team experience, your students will plan a supplemental witness to tell their friends about Jesus by answering three questions:

Question #1: Who is your target?
Question #2: What is your objective or purpose?
Question #3: How do you get there?

2. Target Practice
Checklists keep us organized and efficient and ultimately help us reach our goals. During this D-Team experience, your students will prepare for a supplemental witness by going through a three-point checklist:

Checkpoint #1: Priorities
Checkpoint #2: People
Checkpoint #3: Prayer

Unit 4 Introduction

3. Hit or Miss?

Evaluations bring change and growth. During this D-Team experience, your students will see God's power at work in their lives and in their friends' lives by putting into action two processing values:

Value #1: Debrief the planned supplemental witness.
Value #2: Celebrate the planned supplemental witness.

Unit Memory Verse

"The Lord's hand was with them, and a great number of people believed and turned to the Lord" (Acts 11:21).

Bull's-Eye

1

Before the D-Team Experience

LEADER DEVOTION

Do you remember the first time you shared your faith with someone? What were the circumstances? Was it unexpected, or did you plan for the opportunity? Were you prepared? Do you wish that you could have had something to help make it a little easier to bring up the topic? Something that might have opened the person's mind to your faith?

There are probably some of us who haven't experienced sharing our faith for various reasons. If it is from lack of opportunity or fear of rejection, then today is a new day full of opportunity—take a new step of faith and trust God to use you. He calls all of us to share His Good News. Before you ask your students to prepare an event that will give them an opportunity to share their faith with their friends, you need to reexperience the opportunity to share your faith. Take this challenge before you prepare for this D-Team experience.

LOOKING AHEAD

Student Focus
Targets help us focus on what we are shooting at and ultimately help us hit the bull's-eye. During this D-Team experience, your students will plan an event to use as a supplemental witness to tell their friends about Jesus by answering three questions:

Question #1: Who is your target?
Question #2: What is your objective or purpose?
Question #3: How do you get there?

Unit Memory Verse
"The Lord's hand was with them, and a great number of people believed and turned to the Lord" (Acts 11:21).

Practical Impact
In this D-Team experience, your students will brainstorm an activity that will help them introduce their friends to Jesus Christ. They will use actual targets to help them narrow their ideas down to a "bull's-eye."

BE PREPARED

Materials Needed
- Bibles and pens
- Duplicated Student Notes
- Three large targets labeled Target #1, Target #2, and Target #3 (purchase them at a sporting goods store or make your own with three rings outside the bull's-eye)

Special Preparation

- Prior to this D-Team experience, ask your students to bring their yearbooks or pictures of as many of their seeking, non-Christian friends that they can find.
- Check your calendar for a time to schedule the supplemental witness event. Ideally, you should hold the event between D-Team experiences 2 and 3 of this unit.

Environment

To set up the environment for this D-Team experience, you can choose one of the following. Option 1 works in any setting; Option 2 moves the experience outside your normal setting.

Option 1: Bring as many different kinds of targets that you can find and set them up around the room. You could put a little description under each one to explain what they are for.

Option 2: Take your students to a shooting range or any place that has target practice.

Prep Notes

Leading the D-Team Experience

(60 min. total)

GET STARTED

(5 min.)

Unit Preview

Have a student read aloud the following information from the "Preview" in the Student Notes: ***In Unit 4, you will discover how to evangelize your friends by creating, preparing, and celebrating a supplemental witness.***

Unit Memory Verse

Read aloud Acts 11:21: "The Lord's hand was with them, and a great number of people believed and turned to the Lord." Explain that the "Lord's hand" indicates approval or blessing.

Student Prayer

Have a junior or sophomore in your group pray for focus during this D-Team experience.

Focus

Share with your D-Team members that this week they will create a supplemental witness to tell their friends about Jesus by answering three questions:

Question #1: Who is your target?
Question #2: What is your objective or purpose?
Question #3: How do you get there?

THE EXPERIENCE

(40 min.)

Question #1: Who is your target?

Have your students display their yearbooks or pictures. Now ask them to spend a minute or two silently looking at each of them. Ask: ***Who are the friends that God is putting on your hearts? How do you determine with whom you should share your faith? Are these friends at a point in their lives where they will listen? How do you know?***

Challenge each student to pick one or two friends out of the group of pictures. Put the rest of the pictures away. Then make sure everyone knows the names of the chosen ones. These friends are their targets.

Tell your students that we are going to study an example of Jesus using a supplemental witness to share eternal life with someone who needed it. Have a student ***read aloud John 4:4–7.*** Ask: ***What was the woman's initial need?*** (She needed water.)

Have your students ***read John 4:8–12.*** Then ask: ***How did Jesus bring faith into the conversation?*** (He compared the need for living water—the gift of eternal life—to the need for water that the woman was drawing from the well.)

Ask a student to read aloud John 4:13. Ask: ***How did the woman respond to Jesus' questions?*** (She asked Jesus for the living water that He talked about.
He didn't just push His faith on her; He used a common interest and reached out to

Prep Notes

her with more than just meeting her need.)

Jesus could have probably talked to several different people that day, but He chose to talk to the Samaritan woman. Remind them of who they have chosen to talk to by taking the pictures your students picked out of the group and pinning them up on Target #1.

Question #2: What is your objective or purpose?
Jesus was intentional and knew the woman's needs. His purpose in talking with the woman at the well was to provide her with eternal life. What is your purpose? What do you want your friends to walk away with? (Suggestions: a taste of Jesus' love, forgiveness, or compassion; new relationships; breaking down barriers to Christianity; a relationship with Jesus Christ.) To get your students thinking, ask questions like: What do your target friends need to hear right now? What will your friends go home thinking about? Don't discount any suggestion—take each one and then pick one on which the majority agrees.

After coming up with a purpose, have a student pin it or write it on Target #2 in the bull's-eye.

Question #3: How do you get there?
Say: ***Targets have three to four rings around the bull's-eye. Now, we must figure out each ring that leads to the center.***

Take a look at Target #1 (with the photos of friends) with your students. Ask them: ***What would help these friends be more open to hearing the message that is written on Target #2?*** (A movie? Music? A sporting event? A cookout? A game night? Scavenger hunt? Visiting a cemetery?) The supplemental witness has to be something that will appeal to your friends, not necessarily to you. Make this choice quickly by allowing two to three minutes to brainstorm ideas. Then ask your students to choose one idea. Save the rest of the ideas for future times. Write the chosen idea on the outermost ring of Target #3.

Ask: ***What kinds of activities will move us closer to the bull's-eye or purpose?*** Suggest that the next ring on the target could be a video clip, a question, or a song that will help their friends open up to hearing the message in the bull's-eye. Write the chosen activities on the rings closer to the bulls-eye.

The last step toward the bull's-eye is a personal testimony from one of your students. This is going to be uncomfortable for some of your students, but don't eliminate anyone without his or her permission. Ask your D-Team members: ***Who could give a personal testimony?*** Put the chosen person's name in the ring closest to the bull's-eye.

(5 min.)

REFLECTION

Take the next five minutes to look back over the plans on the target. Address any logistical issues, like when and where to hold the event. (Ideally, the event will take place after your next D-Team experience.)

Give your students a few moments to record honest responses to the following questions found in their Student Notes: ***What was most meaningful to you about our experience today? What does God want you to do in response?***

Ask a student to read aloud the Summary Statements in the Student Notes.

Prep Notes

Summary Statements

We learned today that . . .
- Jesus was intentional with His witnessing.
- Your friends need Jesus.
- You can be creative in sharing your faith with your friends.

MAKE AN IMPACT

(10 min.)

. . . In Your Life

The next step for your students is to start contacting their target friends and begin asking them to come with them to your special event. They also need to be prepared to do some work during the week to make their event happen. Help students divide up the responsibilities for the event.

. . . With Accountability

Have your D-Team members form pairs to become accountability partners for the week and to work on the memory verse. Have each student begin learning the **Unit Memory Verse** by writing it out in the space provided in the Student Notes.

Prayer

Bring the students back together and close in prayer.

name	phone

Begin learning your memory verse by writing it out in the space below.

MEMORY VERSE

Acts 11:21

1. Bull's-Eye

Preview
In Unit 4 you will discover how to evangelize your friends by creating, preparing, and celebrating a supplemental witness.

Unit Memory Verse
"The Lord's hand was with them, and a great number of people believed and turned to the Lord" (Acts 11:21).

Focus
This week, you will create a supplemental witness to tell your friends about Jesus by answering three questions.

THE EXPERIENCE

Question #1: Who is your target?
Who are the friends that God is putting on your heart?

How do you determine with whom you should share your faith?

Are these friends at a point in their lives where they will listen? How do you know?

Read John 4:4–7. What was the woman's initial need?

Read John 4:8–12. How did Jesus bring faith into the conversation?

Read John 4:13. How did the woman respond to Jesus' questions?

Question #2: What is your objective or purpose?
Jesus was intentional and knew the woman's needs. His purpose in talking with the woman at the well was to provide her with eternal life. What is your purpose? What do you want your friends to walk away with?

Question #3: How do you get there?
Targets have three to four rings around the bulls-eye. Now we must figure out each ring that leads to the center.

Outer ring: What would help your friends be more open to hearing the message that is written on Target #2?

Middle ring: What kinds of activities will move us closer to the bull's-eye or purpose?

Inner ring: Who could give a personal testimony?

REFLECTION

What was most meaningful to you about our experience today?

What does God want you to do in response?

Summary Statements

We learned today that . . .

- Jesus was intentional with His witnessing.
- Your friends need Jesus.
- You can be creative in sharing your faith with your friends.

MAKE AN IMPACT

. . . In Your Life
The next step is to start contacting your target friends and begin asking them to come to your special event. Be prepared to do some work during the week to make your event happen. Write down your specific assignment in the space below.

. . . With Accountability
With your accountability partner, talk about your responses to the "Reflection" questions and exchange phone numbers. Call each other this week to hold each other accountable to making an impact in your life.

Target Practice

2

Before the D-Team Experience

LEADER DEVOTION

Have you ever taken the time to study John the Baptist's life? He spent his ministry preparing the way for Jesus to come and change the lives of stubborn people. Read John 1:6–9 and Luke 7:18–28. John acknowledges that he is here to turn people toward God. In Luke 7:27, John is portrayed as the one sent to prepare the way. What a calling! In a sense, we are all called to be John the Baptists. We are to prepare the way for Jesus to change the lives of the people around us. In the midst of planning this supplemental witness, slow down enough to see that you are preparing the way for Jesus to come and change the lives of your students' friends. Pray that God will keep that foremost in your heart.

LOOKING AHEAD

Student Focus
Every D-Team member will prepare for a supplemental witness by going through a three-point checklist:

Checkpoint #1: People
Checkpoint #2: Prayer
Checkpoint #3: Priorities

Unit Memory Verse
"The Lord's hand was with them, and a great number of people believed and turned to the Lord" (Acts 11:21).

Practical Impact
Each student will walk home with a checklist in hand that will help him or her to complete the responsibilities for the supplemental witness event and stay focused on the target.

BE PREPARED

Materials Needed

- Bibles and pens
- Duplicated Student Notes
- Targets from the last D-Team experience
- Dartboard and darts (Option 1)
- Amy Grant's *Songs from the Loft* CD or cassette tape
- CD or tape player

Special Preparation

Ideally, your supplemental witness event is scheduled to take place after this D-Team experience, but before the next D-Team experience. Double-check the dates so you can remind students of the schedule of events.

Environment

To set up the environment for this D-Team experience, you can choose one of the following. Option 1 works in any setting; Option 2 moves the experience outside your normal setting.

Option 1: Set up a dartboard and let your students take a few close-range shots to get the idea of target practice.

Option 2: Have your students try some type of target practice by setting up a big target on the ground and setting a boundary for your students to throw rocks to try to hit it.

Prep Notes

Leading the D-Team Experience

(60 min. total)

GET STARTED

(5 min.)

Review

Have a student read aloud the information under "Review" in the Student Notes: ***Last week you developed a supplemental witness event that you will be carrying out soon. You took on an assignment to begin preparing for the event. What progress have you made?***

Student Prayer

Have each older student in your group pray for the supplemental witness event and the friends you hope to reach.

Focus

Share with your group that during this D-Team experience, they will prepare for a supplemental witness by going through a three-point checklist:

Checkpoint #1: People
Checkpoint #2: Prayer
Checkpoint #3: Priorities

THE EXPERIENCE

(40 min.)

During this unit, you have been working on sharing your faith with your friends by developing a supplemental witness to prepare the way for Jesus to change lives. Today you will finalize the details, but all of you will accomplish something much greater. You will prepare yourselves spiritually for this event.

Begin this experience with an explanation of why target practice is very important. Tell your students that they cannot expect to do something with excellence without putting in some practice, even if it is a minimum amount. Ask: ***What are some examples of things you have to practice if you want to do them well?*** Point out that practice helps us take checks on what we can and can't do. It also helps us discover what areas need the most work. Tell them that today we will be target practicing. Our first checkpoint will be in the area of people.

Checkpoint #1: People

Explain that sometimes we get so caught up in planning an event, that we temporarily forget the reason we are planning it in the first place. Remind your D-Team members that ultimately they want their friends to come to know Jesus in a personal way.

Have a student ***read aloud 1 Corinthians 10:33–11:1.*** Ask: ***What was Paul trying to tell his readers?***

Refer back to Target #1 and ask: ***How are you doing with asking your target friends to come to the event you have planned? Have you asked all of them? Are they excited? Discouraged? Who's coming?*** Talk about each picture on the target. Ask if anyone else needs help with the more reluctant guests.

Prep Notes

Checkpoint #2: Prayer
Say: ***Checkpoint #2 goes hand in hand with Checkpoint #1. Have you been praying for your friends? Are you praying for open minds and hearts? Are you asking God to bless the event and create changes in the lives of those who attend?***

Assign each student one of the following passages: ***Matthew 18:20; 21:22; Philippians 4:6; James 1:6; 5:16.*** Ask your students: ***Share what these verses have to do with preparing a supplemental witness.*** Point out that each passage emphasizes that we should seek God's hand in everything that we do.

Take the next ten minutes to pray together. Put the pictures of your target friends in the middle and pray for each person. Ask if there are any specific prayer requests, and then have several or all of your students pray. Encourage them to be bold in asking God to do a great work in their friends' hearts.

If, after going through Checkpoints #1 and #2, you feel as though your students need to spend more time in these two areas, spend some time asking questions and encouraging them to continue pursuing their friends.

Checkpoint #3: Priorities
Checkpoint #3 will help your D-Team members assess their event and come up with things that need to be done before it actually takes place. This is called target practice. Here are some general details that may help your D-Team members as they complete their plans:

Event date—Confirm with everyone.
Invitations—Check to see that they have been sent (via mail or phone).
Food—Confirm who is buying and setting it up.
Transportation—Has it been arranged for underclassmen?
Music—Has it been selected and screened?
Turning question before the testimony—What question will the whole event focus on and answer for the guests?
Testimony—Who will tie in the event to his or her life? Have you and the D-Team members heard the testimony yet?
Closure to the evening—You could have a student pray, but don't spring it on him or her at the last minute in front of friends.
Other—Fill in the details that fit your particular event.

Remind your students that this is their event and that you, the leader, are simply the facilitator. Encourage all of your students to particpate in some way. Ask:

- Which detail woul you like to take care of?
- What do you need to do this week to fulfill that responsibility?
- Do you need help?
- How can you make preparing for the event a priority?

Have each student write down his or her responsibility in the space provided on the Student Notes.

(5 min.)

REFLECTION

Today, your students took some time to prepare for an event that could change the outlook on one of their friend's eternity. The event itself is not what will make the difference; it will be through prayer and your students having an open heart to be used by God to bring their friends into the kingdom. Play a recording of Amy Grant's

Prep Notes

"Hope Set High" (*Songs from the Loft,* 1993, Word) to guide the students' silent reflection.

Give your students a few moments to record honest responses to the following questions found in their Student Notes: ***What was most meaningful to you about our experience today? What does God want you to do in response?***

Ask a student to read aloud the Summary Statements in the Student Notes.

Summary Statements

We learned today that . . .

- People are the reason for all the planning and work that goes into a supplemental witness.
- Prayer will be the tool that will invite God to do the life-changing work in a heart.
- Working as a team is God's priority for the church to reach their friends.

MAKE AN IMPACT

(10 min.)

. . . In Your Life

Ask your students to follow through on the responsibilities they wrote in their Student Notes. Challenge them to commit to praying five minutes daily for changed hearts in their friends. And urge them to make a follow-up contact with the friends they've invited.

. . . With Accountability

Have the D-Team members form pairs to become accountability partners for the week and to work on the memory verse. Have each student write out the **Unit Memory Verse** and recite it to a partner.

Prayer

Bring the students back together and close with prayer.

Summary Statements

We learned today that . . .

- People are the reason for all the planning and work that goes into a supplemental witness.
- Prayer will be the tool that will invite God to do the life-changing work in a heart.
- Working as a team is God's priority for the church to reach their friends.

MAKE AN IMPACT

. . . In Your Life
Follow through on the responsibilities you recorded above. Commit to praying five minutes daily for changed hearts in your friends. And be sure to make a follow-up contact with the friend you invited to the event.

. . . With Accountability
With your accountability partner, talk about your responses to the "Reflection" questions. Exchange phone numbers. Call each other this week to hold each other accountable to making an impact in your life.

name	phone

Review your memory verse by writing it out in the space below. Then recite it to your partner.

MEMORY VERSE

Acts 11:32

2. Target Practice

Review
Last week you developed a supplemental witness event that you will be carrying out soon. You took on an assignment to begin preparing for the event. What progress have you made?

Focus
This week, you will prepare for a supplemental witness by going through a three-point checklist.

THE EXPERIENCE

What are some examples of things you have to practice if you want to do them well?

Checkpoint #1: People
Read 1 Corinthians 10:33–11:1. What was Paul trying to tell his readers?

How are you doing with asking your target friends to come to the event you have planned? Have you asked all of them? Are they excited? Discouraged? Who's coming?

Checkpoint #2: Prayer
Checkpoint #2 goes hand in hand with Checkpoint #1. Have you been

praying for your friends? Are you praying for open minds and hearts? Are you asking God to bless the event and create changes in the lives of those who attend?

Read your assigned passage and be prepared to share what your verses have to do with preparing a supplemental witness:

Matthew 18:20

Matthew 21:22

Philippians 4:6

James 1:6

James 5:16

Take the next ten minutes to pray together. Put the pictures of your target friends in the middle of your circle and pray for each person.

Checkpoint #3: Priorities
Checkpoint #3 will help you assess your event and come up with things that need to be done before it actually takes place. This is called target practice.

In the space below, record some general details that may help you as you complete your plans:

Event date—Confirm with everyone.
Invitations—Check to see that they have been sent (via mail or phone).
Food—
Transportation—
Music—
Turning question before the testimony—
Testimony—
Closure to the evening—
Other—

Today, you took some time to prepare for an event that could change the outlook on one of your friend's eternity. The next step for you will be to take a check on your responsibilities for the planned event. Record your role for the event in the space below.

REFLECTION

What was most meaningful to you about our experience today?

What does God want you to do in response?

Hit or Miss?

3

Before the D-Team Experience

LEADER DEVOTION

We live in such a fast-paced world that we don't always slow down enough to celebrate the great things God is doing in and through us. Imagine everyone in heaven throwing a big party when the Gospel is shared with a lost person! Slow down enough to celebrate in your own quietness. Take time to worship and praise God for using you and your D-Team members to shine the light of Jesus into a dark and dying world. Celebrate!

LOOKING AHEAD

Student Focus
Evaluations bring change and growth. Every D-Team member will see God's power at work in his or her life and their friends' lives by putting into action two processing values:

Value #1: Debrief the planned supplemental witness.
Value #2: Celebrate the planned supplemental witness.

Unit Memory Verse
"The Lord's hand was with them, and a great number of people believed and turned to the Lord" (Acts 11:21).

Practical Impact
Your students will receive a small target on which they will record where they "hit" with their targeted friend. It will remind them to celebrate hits, and to strive to do better with the misses.

BE PREPARED

Materials Needed
- Bibles and pens
- Duplicated Student Notes
- Party supplies: balloons, music, food, streamers, etc.
- A small target for each student
- Slips of paper or notecards

Special Preparation
- Previous to this D-Team experience, your D-Team members should have carried out their plan to do a supplemental witness event that helped them introduce their friends to Jesus. This D-Team experience is designed as a follow-up to that event. If you have not held your supplemental witness event yet, you can use this experience to study how to evaluate an event, but you will have to make some adjustments. Be sure to study the session thoroughly.

- Your D-Team can celebrate in a number of different ways. They could worship and sing together. They could take the Lord's Supper together to celebrate what God has done for everyone. They could share success stories. They could build an altar of some type to remember what God has done. Select a way that is appropriate for your students and make any necessary preparations.

Environment

To set up the environment for this D-Team experience, you can choose one of the following. Option 1 works in any setting; Option 2 moves the experience outside your normal setting.

Option 1: Decorate your meeting area for a big party and celebration. Use balloons, food, music—anything that will create the atmosphere of a party.

Option 2: Take your D-Team members any place that you could throw a big party—a park, a restaurant, someone's backyard.

Prep Notes

Leading the D-Team Experience

(60 min. total)

GET STARTED

(5 min.)

Review

Have a student read aloud the information under "Review" in the Student Notes: ***Last time you developed checklists that would help you in preparing for your supplemental witness event. You were challenged to write down your role in helping make the event happen. You were also challenged to pray five minutes a day for heart change to start in your friends. Share with the group how this went.***

Student Prayer

Ask the student who gave his or her testimony at your special event to pray, asking God to join the students in celebrating what happened in their friends' lives.

Focus

Share with your group that during this D-Team experience they will see God's power at work in their lives and their friends' lives by putting into action two processing values:

Value #1: Debrief the planned supplemental witness.
Value #2: Celebrate the planned supplemental witness.

THE EXPERIENCE

(40 min.)

Have your room or area prepared for a party with music playing when your students arrive. Allow them the freedom to mingle and talk together for the first ten or fifteen minutes. Let them laugh and enjoy each other. Then bring your D-Team members together and sit down on the floor or on the ground.

Value #1: Debrief the planned supplemental witness.

Tell the group that you are going to spend the next few minutes getting feedback on your event. Open the discussion up for anyone to share. Instruct them to give one positive comment and one comment about something they would do differently next time. If your students do not respond, share something yourself or ask a student to begin and then go around the circle. You could ask them to evaluate each ring on the target (the activities that made up the event—from the music to the testimony to the conversations that followed).

Write each positive comment on slips of paper or notecards that you can hand out during the prayer time. Hand out the small targets and ask your students to take a moment to make a personal evaluation of how close they got to the bull's-eye with their friends.

Ask: ***Would you do this event again? What did your friends think of it? What were the conversations like that followed afterward? What did you learn personally about yourself? About your friend? What prayers were answered?***

Value #2: Celebrate the planned supplemental witness.

After you have debriefed for a little while, make a transition into a celebration by

Prep Notes

reading aloud Luke 15:1–10. Then read verses 7 and 10 again. Ask: ***What did God take time to do? Why was He celebrating?*** Explain that if God takes the time to celebrate spiritual victories, then we should take the time to celebrate also. Take time to celebrate together in a way your students will find meaningful. They could worship and sing together, take the Lord's Supper together to celebrate what God has done for everyone, share success stories, or build an altar of some type to remember what God has done.

(5 min.)

REFLECTION

Your students have taken time to debrief and celebrate who God is and what He has done. The next step is to go to God in prayer and thank Him. Choose one of the following options:

- Hand out the notecards with the positive feedback for your students to thank God for during the prayer time.
- Pray for each student who came to the event and the ones who were not able to come.
- Praise God for using your D-Team members to share the Good News of Jesus with their friends.
- Ask your students what they are thankful for.

Allow your prayer time to be open for everyone to have a chance to pray if they want to participate.

Give your students a few moments to record honest responses to the following questions found in their Student Notes: ***What was most meaningful to you about our experience today? What does God want you to do in response?***

Ask a student to read aloud the Summary Statements in the Student Notes.

Summary Statements

We learned today that . . .

- God is the one who does the work in our hearts.
- Luke 15 shows us that our Father celebrates in heaven.
- We need to give God all the honor and glory for what is accomplished spiritually in our friends' hearts.

(10 min.)

MAKE AN IMPACT

. . . In Your Life

Going public is a big step for some of your students. Challenge them to make follow-up phone calls or get together with their target friends. Ask your students to be intentional with their conversations—don't just get together and talk; ask specific questions. You may need to help them figure out what a good question would be for their friends.

Last of all, ask your students if any of their friends would like to come to your next D-Team experience. If so, then challenge your students to talk to their friends about taking the next step in their lives.

. . . With Accountability

Have the D-Team members form pairs to become accountability partners for the week and to work on the memory verse. Have each student write out the **Unit Memory Verse**, recite it to his or her partner, and share a way the verse is meaningful in his or her life.

Prayer

Bring the students back together and close in prayer.

Prep Notes

"Reflection" questions and exchange phone numbers. Call each other this week to hold each other accountable to making an impact in your life.

name	phone

Review your memory verse by writing it out in the space below. After reciting it to your partner, share a way the verse is meaningful in your life.

MEMORY VERSE
Acts 11:21

3. Hit or Miss?

Review
Last time you developed checklists that would help you in preparing for your D-Team's event. You were challenged to write down your role in helping make the event happen. You were also challenged to pray five minutes a day for heart change to start in your friends. Share with the group how this went.

Focus
During this D-Team experience, you will see God's power at work in your life and your friends' lives by putting into action two processing values.

THE EXPERIENCE

Value #1: Debrief the planned supplemental witness.
Spend the next few minutes offering feedback on your supplemental witness event. Give one positive comment and one comment about something you would do differently next time.

Would you do this event again?

What did your friends think of it?

What were the conversations like that followed afterward?

What did you learn personally about yourself? About your friend?

What prayers were answered?

Value #2: Celebrate the planned supplemental witness.
Read Luke 15:1–10. Then read verses 7 and 10 again. What did God take time to do?

Why was He celebrating?

REFLECTION

The next step is to go to God in prayer and thank Him. Choose one of the following options:

- Use the notecards with the positive feedback to thank God for during the prayer time.
- Pray for each student who came to the event and the ones who were not able to come.
- Praise God for using you to share the Good News of Jesus with your friends.
- Share what you are thankful for.

What was most meaningful to you about our experience today?

What does God want you to do in response?

Summary Statements

We learned today that . . .

- God is the one who does the work in our hearts.
- Luke 15 shows us that our Father celebrates in heaven.
- We need to give God all the honor and glory for what is accomplished spiritually in our friends' hearts.

MAKE AN IMPACT

. . . In Your Life
Going public is a big step for some of you. Make follow-up phone calls or get together with your target friends. Be intentional with your conversations—don't just get together and talk; ask specific questions. You may need to figure out what a good question would be for your friends. Last of all, ask your friends if they would like to come to your next experience.

. . . With Accountability
With your accountability partner, talk about your responses to the

Shepherding Summary Form

Complete this form immediately after every meeting and give a copy to your ministry director or small groups coordinator.

ATTENDANCE

Leader:

Apprentice leader:

Members present:

Members absent:

Guests filling the "empty chair":

Starting core number:

ACTIVITY SUMMARY

Briefly describe how you incorporated the CLEAR values listed below.

Christ—How was Christ made the central focus of your time together?

Listen— Were you able to meet the students' needs to be heard? What concerns arose?

Empty chair—Are students praying for specific friends they could invite to join the small group? How are you fostering an openness to new members?

Affirm—In what ways were you able to affirm your students?

Read and pray—How effective was your time in the Word and in prayer together?

CELEBRATION

What's happening in your small group that you'd like to celebrate or note? What problems or questions do you need help with?

WILLOW CREEK RESOURCES

This resource was created to serve you.

It is just one of many ministry tools that are part of the Willow Creek Resources® line, published by the Willow Creek Association together with Zondervan Publishing House. The Willow Creek Association was created in 1992 to serve a rapidly growing number of churches from all across the denominational spectrum that are committed to helping unchurched people become fully devoted followers of Christ. There are now more than 2,500 WCA member churches worldwide.

The Willow Creek Association links like-minded leaders with each other and with strategic vision, information, and resources in order to build prevailing churches. Here are some of the ways it does that:

- **Church Leadership Conferences**—3 1/2 -day events, held at Willow Creek Community Church in South Barrington, IL, that are being used by God to help church leaders find new and innovative ways to build prevailing churches that reach unchurched people.
- **The Leadership Summit**—a once-a-year event designed to increase the leadership effectiveness of pastors, ministry staff, volunteer church leaders, and Christians in business.
- **Willow Creek Resources®**—to provide churches with a trusted channel of ministry resources in areas of leadership, evangelism, spiritual gifts, small groups, drama, contemporary music, and more. For more information, call Willow Creek Resources® at 800/876-7335. Outside the US call 610/532-1249.
- ***WCA News***—a bimonthly newsletter to inform you of the latest trends, resources, and information on WCA events from around the world.
- ***The Exchange***—our classified ads publication to assist churches in recruiting key staff for ministry positions.
- **The Church Associates Directory**—to keep you in touch with other WCA member churches around the world.
- ***WillowNet***—an Internet service that provides access to hundreds of Willow Creek messages, drama scripts, songs, videos and multimedia suggestions. The system allows users to sort through these elements and download them for a fee.
- ***Defining Moments***—a monthly audio journal for church leaders, in which Lee Strobel asks Bill Hybels and other Christian leaders probing questions to help you discover biblical principles and transferable strategies to help maximize your church's potential.

For conference and membership information please write or call:

Willow Creek Association
P.O. Box 3188
Barrington, IL 60011-3188
ph: (847) 765-0070
fax: (847) 765-5046
www.willowcreek.org

0597